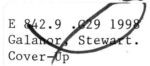

COVER-UP

COVER-UP

by STEWART GALANOR

Kestrel Books
New York

Kestrel Books
134 West 93 Street
New York, NY 10025

Library of Congress Catalog Card Number: 94-012045

ISBN 0-9662772-0-1

Cover: Zapruder film, frame 269 electronically sharpened

For Nancy

CONTENTS

Walt Sisco, The Dallas Morning News

NOVEMBER 1963

On Friday, November 22, 1963, President John F. Kennedy rode in a motorcade procession through Dallas, Texas.

Abraham Zapruder

At 12:30 in the afternoon, as the Presidential limousine proceeded down Elm Street in Dealey Plaza, shots were fired. President Kennedy was struck in the throat.

Abraham Zapruder

And seconds later . . .

Abraham Zapruder

a bullet tore apart his head.

The motorcade sped to Parkland Hospital, where at 1 p.m. the President was pronounced dead.

Cecil Stoughton, Lyndon Baines Johnson Library

An hour later on the Presidential plane, Lyndon Johnson was sworn in as the 36th president of the United States.

Photographer Unknown

That afternoon police arrested Lee Harvey Oswald as a suspect in the murder.

The next morning the Dallas Police announced that the case had
been solved: Oswald, acting alone, had shot President Kennedy
from a sixth floor window of the Texas School Book Depository
Building, where a rifle and three cartridges were found.

Oswald, however, maintained he was innocent. "I'm just a patsy," he said.

The assassination of President Kennedy provoked speculation: Was Oswald indeed a lone assassin? Was he involved in a conspiracy to kill the President? Was he a hired killer acting for someone else? Was he innocent?

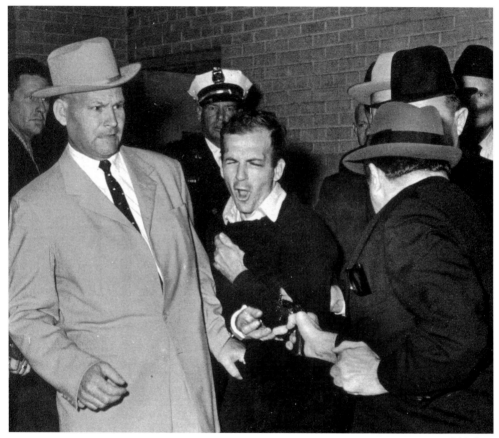

Then on Sunday morning, November 24, while millions watched on TV, Oswald was murdered in the basement of a Dallas jail by Jack Ruby, the owner of a Dallas strip-tease joint called the Carousel. Rumors spread rapidly, and a shocked nation demanded answers.

Representative Gerald Ford, Representative Hale Boggs, Senator Richard Russell, Chief Justice Earl Warren, Senator John Sherman Cooper, Former World Bank President John J. McCloy, Former CIA Director Allen Dulles. *National Archives*

On Friday, November 29, Lyndon Johnson formed a commission charged with investigating the assassination of President Kennedy. Almost immediately it was called the Warren Commission, after the Chief Justice of the United States, Earl Warren, who was its chairman.

On September 24, 1964, after ten months of secret hearings, Chief Justice Earl Warren presented the Commission's report to President Johnson. The Commission found that Oswald, acting alone, had assassinated President Kennedy. Mainstream media hailed it as "the most massive, detailed and convincing piece of detective work ever undertaken, unmatched in the annals of fact finding."

David Anderson

Two months later the U. S. Government released 26 volumes of testimony and exhibits which contained the evidence on which the Warren Report was purportedly based.

The New York Times reported that the 26 Volumes "overwhelmingly supported the conclusions [of the Warren Commission's Report] that the assassination was no conspiracy but the work of one unhappy man, Lee Harvey Oswald."

Most Americans, however, continued to believe there was a conspiracy to assassinate the President.

CASE NOT CLOSED

The assassination of President John F. Kennedy is a seminal event in American history. Contrary to conventional wisdom, the trust Americans once had in their national government to tell the truth began to decline not with the Vietnam War or the Watergate scandal but with the assassination. Most Americans simply do not believe their government's version of what happened—that one lone communist malcontent murdered Kennedy.

The reluctance of our government to pursue a special investigation compounded the mystery surrounding the President's death. After Ruby murdered Oswald, the District Attorney of Dallas announced that Oswald was guilty "without any doubt, to a moral certainty" and declared the case closed. The next day, in a phone conversation with FBI director J. Edgar Hoover, President Johnson crudely argued, "We can't be checking up on every shooting scrap in the country." (Phone Conversation with Hoover, November 25, 1963, National Archives) Four days later, however, to dispel mounting public suspicions of a conspiracy, Johnson created the Warren Commission.

Over the last four decades the major news media have made numerous attempts to defend the Warren Commission's Report. Each undertaking has failed to influence public opinion, serving only to deepen suspicions about a plot and to foster cynicism and a loss of respect for our institutions of government. A CBS poll taken in October 1993 found that close to 90 percent of Americans surveyed believed there was a conspiracy; almost 50 percent thought the CIA was involved; 80 percent believed there was an official cover-up. ("Who Killed JFK? The Final Chapter," *CBS News*, November 22, 1993)

This book presents the evidence of a conspiracy to assassinate President Kennedy and documents the disturbing measures taken by our government and major news media to cover it up. Virtually all of this evidence was gathered by the Dallas Police and agencies of the United States Government and is published in the Warren Commission's *26 Volumes of Testimony and Exhibits* or stored in the National Archives. Although the evidence of a conspiracy is overwhelming, this book makes no attempt to speculate on who killed Kennedy.

The history of the cover-up begins with a problem that faced the FBI immediately after the assassination and that later taxed all the prosecutorial skills of the Warren Commission.

MEDICAL EVIDENCE

After President Kennedy was shot, he was rushed to Dallas's Parkland Hospital. There, in a hopeless attempt to save his life, doctors performed a tracheotomy. Although the President appeared dead, they administered blood and performed cardiac massage. But these efforts failed, for his brain had been destroyed. He was pronounced dead at 1 p.m. His body was flown to Washington, and that evening at Bethesda Naval Hospital in Maryland an autopsy was performed.

AN ENTRANCE WOUND

When President Kennedy arrived at the Parkland Hospital emergency room, doctors observed a wound in the President's throat and noted its appearance and approximate dimensions. A tracheotomy was performed by making an incision directly through the wound in the neck. This procedure enlarged the hole in the President's neck and obscured the original bullet wound.

At a press conference held that afternoon at Parkland Hospital, Dr. Malcolm Perry, the physician who performed the tracheotomy, said, "There was an entrance wound in the neck." (Transcript 1327-C of Perry and Clark News Conference, November 22, 1963, LBJ Library) As another attending physician, Dr. Ronald Jones, later testified, "The hole [in the throat] was very small and relatively clean cut, as you would see in a bullet that is entering rather than exiting from a patient." (6H55)

Entrance wounds are small, round puncture wounds, about the size of the diameter of the bullet. Dr. Robert McClelland, another of the attending physicians, explained to the press and later to the Warren Commission that the Parkland doctors knew the difference between an entrance wound and an exit wound. They had the opportunity to examine bullet wounds every day. A bullet characteristically makes a small entrance wound, ruptures tissue inside the body and tears a large, jagged opening as it passes out the other side. Consequently, the Parkland doctors believed the wound in the President's throat was an entrance wound. (Richard Dudman, *The New Republic*, December 21, 1963; 6H36)

THE PROBLEM

Because the evidence indicating that the President was shot from the front and because Oswald was supposedly firing from the Book Depository to the rear, a difficult problem confronted the FBI and the Warren Commission. In essence the problem might be posed as: How did Oswald shoot the President in the front from behind? (See Documents 1 and 2 in the Apprendix, page 121)

Two weeks after the assassination, newspapers reported that federal agents were still reconstructing the crime on film. An open car with a man and a woman in the back seat simulated again and again the ride of the President. The agents wondered "how the President could have received a bullet in the front of the throat from a rifle in the Texas School Book

Depository Building after his car had passed the building." (Joseph Loftus, *The New York Times*, December 6, 1963)

Life magazine in its December 6, 1963, issue gave the first erroneous answer to this question. Under the title "End To Nagging Rumors: The Six Critical Seconds," *Life* posed the problem this way:

> Since by this time the limousine was 50 yards past Oswald and the President's back was turned almost directly to the sniper, it has been hard to understand how the bullet could enter the front of the throat.

Then *Life* assured the nation:

> But the 8 mm film shows the President turning his body far around to the right as he waves to someone in the crowd. His throat is exposed, toward the sniper's nest, just before he clutches it.

The editors of *Life* must have known their explanation was false. Frames from the 8 mm film (the now-famous Zapruder film), which they cited as proof that the President was turned to the rear when the first bullet entered his throat, had appeared in *Life's* previous issue (November 29, 1963). Those Zapruder frames show that the President is not turned to the rear facing the Book Depository, but is, in fact, facing to the right front when he is struck in the throat; then his arms and hands rise to his neck, and he slowly slumps forward before he is hit in the head. (See the Zapruder film, MPI Home Video, Chicago)

After *Life's* story was exposed as false, it became the Warren Commission's task to answer this nagging question: How could Oswald shoot the President in the

front from behind? What could the Commission do?
With the Commission publicly committed to the theory
that Oswald was lurking at the sixth floor window,
there was only one way to resolve this question.

GOATSKIN TEST

If Oswald was going to be the assassin and do it
alone from the Book Depository, the entrance wound in
the throat must become an exit wound. But that would
mean the doctors at Parkland were all wrong. Page 91
of the Warren Report:

> Experiments performed by Army Wound
> Ballistics experts . . . showed that under sim-
> ulated conditions entry and exit wounds are
> very similar in appearance.

According to the Commission there was a back wound
all along, discovered at the autopsy in Bethesda,
Maryland. The Parkland doctors didn't notice it
because the President had died before they had time
to examine his back. Thus, since entrance and exit
wounds are similar in appearance, the Parkland doctors were mistaken in originally diagnosing the throat
wound as an entrance wound.

The Army ballistics experts had used goatskins to
simulate the President's neck. The experts lined two
goatskins up, placed a slab of gelatin in between to simulate muscle tissue, and fired a bullet through them.
The test was repeated with horsemeat and goatmeat, in
turn, replacing the slab of gelatin. Commission Exhibit
850, found buried in the 26 Volumes of evidence on
page 846 of Volume 17, shows the results of these tests.
(Document 3) The entrance holes are small and round,

with the maximum diameter of the largest hole not exceeding 6 mm. The exit holes, on the other hand, are three times larger, irregular, elongated, in two cases stellate, and measure on the average 8 by 12 mm.

Now how did the Parkland doctors describe the wound they observed in the President's throat before the tracheotomy was performed? Dr. Perry testified before the Warren Commission that the wound was "between 3 and 5 mm in size." (6H15) Dr. Baxter said the wound was "4 to 5 mm in widest diameter . . . the size of the wound is measured by the hole plus the damaged skin around the area, so that it was a very small wound." (6H42) Dr. Carrico said it was "probably a 4 to 7 mm wound" and had "no jagged edges or stellate lacerations." (6H3) Dr. Jones described the throat wound as "no larger than a quarter of an inch in diameter [6 mm] . . . There appeared to be relatively smooth edges around the wound . . . it was a very small, smooth wound." (6H54)

As hard as it is to believe, the Commission failed to show the Parkland doctors the goatskins and ask them which set of wounds, either the entrance or exit wounds, resembled the wound they had seen. From the doctors' descriptions it is reasonable to assume they would have picked the set of entrance wounds. Despite the Warren Commission's assurances to the contrary, even an untrained eye can distinguish between the entrance and exit wounds on the goatskins.

WHERE WERE THE WOUNDS?

It should have been a simple matter to locate the President's wounds. There was, after all, an autopsy. But in the course of just a few months the locations of the wounds underwent curious transformations.

VERSION ONE — FBI REENACTMENT

When the FBI conducted a reenactment of the assassination for the Warren Commission in May of 1964, it placed the back wound slightly to the right of the spine and about six inches below the top of the collar. (Document 4) There was substantial support for the location of the back wound. The autopsy description sheet filled out during the autopsy placed it there. (Document 5) The President's jacket and shirt each had a hole about six inches below the collar. (Documents 6, 7; 2H365) In addition, Secret Service agent Clinton Hill "saw an opening in the back, about six inches below the neckline," when he viewed the President's body in the morgue after the autopsy. (2H143) Furthermore, the Death Certificate made out by Dr. George Burkley, the White House physician, reported that "a second wound occurred in the posterior back at about the level of the third thoracic vertebra." (Document 8)

VERSION TWO — WARREN COMMISSION

But this location for the back wound created a real problem for the Commission. The path of the bullet appeared to be rising upward from back to front, which is inconsistent with a shot from above and behind and provides further evidence of a shot from the front. This inconsistency gave rise to another nagging question: How did Oswald shoot the President from below from above? The Commission never answered this question. Instead, it simply decided that the wound must be located higher. Astonishingly, the Commission came to this conclusion without ever examining the autopsy X-rays and photographs. Earl Warren decided to withhold the X-rays and photographs from the Commission because they were too shocking. In his memoirs Warren related,

> "I saw the pictures when they came from Bethesda Naval Hospital, and they were so horrible that I could not sleep well for nights. Accordingly, in order to prevent them from getting into the hands of sensa- tionmongers, I suggested that they not be used by the Commission . . ." (*The Memoirs of Earl Warren*, page 371)

While arguably Warren's suppression of the photographs was justifiable, what possible argument could preclude an examination of the X-rays?

In place of the autopsy X-rays and photographs, the Commission substituted three drawings made by an artist guided by Dr. James Humes, the chief pathologist of the autopsy. (Documents 9, 10, 11) The back wound was moved up to the base of the neck. Now the trajectory conveniently conformed with the path of a bullet shot from above. (Compare the Autopsy Description Sheet filled out during the autopsy, where the back wound is below the neck, Document 5, with the Warren Commission's drawings, made three months after the autopsy, where the wound is at the base of the neck, Documents 9, 10, 11)

VERSION THREE — CLARK PANEL

In 1968 Attorney General Ramsey Clark convened a panel of four distinguished doctors to examine the autopsy X-rays and photographs. The Clark Panel Report was released in January 1969 and disclosed that the wound had moved again. The back wound fell two inches below a fold in the skin at the base of the President's neck, two inches lower than where the autopsy pathologists had placed it in the Warren Commission

Drawings. (Compare Documents 10 and 12) But according to the Clark Panel, it was still anatomically higher than the throat wound. (*Clark Panel Report*, page 9)

VERSION FOUR — HOUSE SELECT COMMITTEE ON ASSASSINATIONS

In 1977 Dr. Michael Baden, the chief forensic pathologist for the House Select Committee on Assassinations (HSCA), differed with the Clark Panel finding. Dr. Baden determined from an examination of the autopsy X-rays and photographs that the back wound was at the level of the first thoracic vertebra. This location, according to the House Committee Medical Panel, meant the back wound was anatomically lower than the throat wound. (Document 13; 1HSCA231,377)

With the House Committee's finding that the back wound was lower than the throat wound, an old problem recurred. The path of the bullet through the neck from back to front would have had to be rising. Again that nagging question: How did Oswald shoot the President from below from above? As Dr. Baden explained once on *NOVA*:

> "The bullet path through President Kennedy's back and neck, indeed, was in the anatomical position at somewhat of an upward angle."

Then Dr. Baden theorized:

> "But this is entirely consistent with a bullet trajectory coming from above downward at a 20 degree angle if the President were leaning forward at the time that the bullet struck him in the manner that I am doing." ("Who Shot President Kennedy?," *NOVA*, November 1988)

And here Dr. Baden leaned forward to demonstrate the angle of the President's wounds. To support Dr. Baden's analysis, *NOVA* claimed that their computer simulation of the assassination found that Kennedy must have bent forward just before he was shot in the back. (Document 14) As logically sound as Dr. Baden's reasoning would seem, it fails to consider one important fact: None of the films and photographs of the assassination shows the President leaning forward when he was struck in the throat. In fact, the Zapruder film shows the President sitting erect as he raises his hands to his throat in reaction to being shot. (Document 15)

PATH OF BULLET

The autopsy pathologists at Bethesda failed to dissect the President's neck to track the bullet's path. This was a serious oversight since, by the pathologists' own admission, they did not determine during the autopsy what had happened to the bullet that entered the President's back.

It was not until Dr. Humes, the chief autopsy pathologist, called Parkland Hospital that he discovered that Dr. Perry had obscured the throat wound when he performed the tracheotomy. Dr. Humes told the Warren Commission that "In speaking of that wound in the neck, Dr. Perry told me that before he enlarged it to make the tracheotomy wound it was 'a few millimeters in diameter.'" (2H362) Nevertheless, Dr. Humes concluded that a bullet entered the President's back and exited through the neck.

The physical evidence, however, is not consistent with Dr. Humes' finding that a bullet passed from back to front. If that were true, the size of the bullet holes should get larger, not smaller. The holes in the back of

FATAL WOUND

When the Parkland doctors treated President Kennedy, they observed two wounds, one in the throat and another in the head. At the press conference held the afternoon of the President's death, Dr. Kemp Clark, who pronounced the President dead, said he observed "a large, gaping loss of tissue" located at the "back of his head . . . towards the right side." (Transcript 1327-C of Perry and Clark News Conference, November 22, 1963, LBJ Library) No fewer than nine doctors wrote in their medical reports or testified to the Commission that they remembered observing a large wound in the right rear area of the President's head. (Document 16)

As it turned out, the Parkland doctors' testimony differed substantially from the findings of the Bethesda autopsy. Besides the back wound, the autopsy pathologists supposedly found a small entrance wound at the back of the President's head, right in the region where the Parkland doctors saw a large gaping wound. (Compare Documents 10 and 16) As with the back wound, it has been difficult to pin down the location of this "entrance wound" to the head.

VERSION ONE — FBI REENACTMENT

The FBI, in its reenactment of the assassination for the Warren Commission in May of 1964, placed the "entrance wound" to the head at the President's hair line. (Document 4)

VERSION TWO — WARREN COMMISSION

The three Bethesda autopsy doctors, in their autopsy report and their testimony before the Warren Commission, concluded that the shot to the President's head came from above and behind. The determination that the shot came from above was somewhat speculative; the position of the President was not known since the autopsy doctors had not seen the Zapruder film. The "entrance wound" was placed 2.5 cm to the right and slightly above the external occipital protuberance, that little bump everyone has in the back of the head. (Documents 11, 12)

There was a problem with this location, however. The angle of a line through the head wounds does not match the angle of a shot from the Book Depository, which is roughly 12 degrees. (WR108; WR189) Thus, the Warren Commission drawing has President Kennedy slumping farther over than depicted in the Zapruder film. (Compare Documents 11 and 17)

When the Warren Commission drawing is placed at an angle that matches President Kennedy's position in the Zapruder film just prior to the fatal shot, the path of the shot rises from back to front, a trajectory which is totally inconsistent with a shot from the Book Depository. (Document 18)

VERSION THREE — CLARK PANEL

In 1969 the Clark Panel, which had been convened by Attorney General Ramsey Clark to examine the autopsy X-rays and photographs, revealed in its report that the head "entrance wound" had moved once again, this time rising to four inches above the external occipital protuberance. (Document 19; *Clark Panel Report*, page 12) As suspicious as this higher location might be, it at least appears to be consistent with a shot from above.

CONTRADICTORY EVIDENCE

In September of 1977, the chief autopsy pathologist Dr.
Humes appeared before the House Select Committee on
Assassinations medical panel, headed by Dr. Baden. The
medical panel confronted Dr. Humes with the Clark
Panel finding that the autopsy X-rays and photographs
show an entrance wound in the back of the the head four
inches higher than he had reported at the autopsy. At first
Dr. Humes refused to accept this new location, and said
that it "certainly was not any wound of entrance."
(7HSCA254) But eventually Dr. Humes conceded to the
medical panel that the wound was higher than he had
previously determined. (1HSCA327) The two other
pathologists, Dr. James Boswell and Dr. Pierre Finck,
steadfastly refused to confirm the new location in their
testimony before the House Medical Panel. (7HSCA246;
HSCA Interview of Dr. Finck, 3/11/78, pages 81, 104, National
Archives)

Fourteen years later in an interview for *The Journal of
the American Medical Association* (*JAMA*) Dr. Humes
reverted to his original observation described in the
autopsy report. "The fatal wound was blatantly obvious. The entrance wound was . . . located 2.5
centimeters to the right and slightly above the external
occipital protuberance." (*JAMA*, May 27, 1992, page 2798)

MASSIVE HEAD WOUND

As with the throat and back wounds, the size and
position of the head wounds are significant. The
Parkland doctors saw a large wound in the right rear of
the President's head. (Document 16) The Bethesda
autopsy doctors, however, said there was no large
wound in the right rear of the head. There was a small

entrance wound there instead. The massive head wound was observed higher on the right side of the head. (Documents 10, 11)

The Parkland doctors interpreted the large wound in the back of the President's head as an exit wound which would have been inconsistent with a shot from behind. Dr. Perry told the Boston Globe he observed an exit wound "despite the fact the assassin shot from above down onto the President." (Herbert Black, November 24, 1963) Dr. Jones testified it "appeared to be an exit wound in the posterior portion of the skull." (6H56) Dr. McClelland's initial impression was of a bullet "exiting out the back, to produce the massive injury in the head." (6H35) Dr. Akin said, "I assume that the right occipitalparietal region was the exit." (6H67)

The House Select Committee on Assassinations argued that the Parkland doctors who remember seeing a large wound at the right rear portion of the President's head, instead of the small entrance wound discovered at the autopsy, were all mistaken.

House Select Committee on Assassinations Claim

The "observations of the Parkland doctors are incorrect"; (7HSCA39) "their recollections were not based on careful examination of the wounds." (7HSCA37)

Evidence

Two Parkland doctors, however, Kemp Clark and Robert McClelland, took the time to examine the wound carefully. Dr. McClelland testified before the Warren Commission, "As I took the position at the head of the table . . . I was in such a position that I could very closely examine the head wound, and I noted that the right posterior portion of the skull had been extremely blasted. . . . you could actually look down into the skull cavity itself and see that probably a third or so, at least, of the brain tissue, posterior cerebral tissue and some of the cerebellar tissue had been blasted out." (Document 16; 6H33)

When a reporter asked Dr. Clark at the afternoon press conference if he could describe the neck wound, Dr. Clark said, "I was busy with his head wound." (Transcript 1327-C of Perry and Clark News Conference, November 22, 1963, LBJ Library)

Dr. Clark later testified, "I then examined the wound in the back of the President's head. This was a large, gaping wound in the right posterior part, with cerebral and cerebellar tissue being damaged and exposed." (6H20)

Dr. Paul Peters explained to the Commission, "About this time it was noted also that he had no effective heart action and Dr. Perry asked whether he should open the chest and massage the heart. . . . It was pointed out that an examination of the brain had been done. . . . and that open-heart massage would probably not add anything to what had already been done." (6H70)

Nine Parkland doctors wrote in their medical reports or testified to the Commission that they remembered observing a large wound in the right rear area of the President's head. Dr. Jones testified the head wound "was a large defect in the back side of the head." (6H53) Dr. Perry described the President's head wound as "a large avulsive injury of the right occipitalparietal area." (6H11; See Document 20 for the locations of the occipital and parietal bones.) Dr. Akin said, "The back of the right occipitalparietal portion of his head was shattered, with brain substance extruding." (6H65) Dr. Carrico testified, "The wound that I saw was a large gaping wound, located in the right occipitalparietal area." (6H6) Dr. Peters said,

"There was a large defect in the occiput . . . in the right occipitalparietal area."(6H71) Dr. Jenkins, in a report made out on November 22, 1963, wrote, "There was a great laceration on the right side of the head (temporal and occipital), causing a great defect in the skull plate so that there was herniation and laceration of great areas of the brain, even to the extent that the cerebellum had protruded from the wound." (17H15)

House Select Committee on Assassinations Claim

"In disagreement with the observations of the Parkland doctors are the 26 people present at the autopsy. All of those interviewed who attended the autopsy corroborated the general location of the wounds as depicted in the [autopsy] photographs [which do not show a large wound in the right rear portion of the skull]; none had differing accounts." (Document 12, 7HSCA37)

Evidence

When the House Committee dissolved in 1979, it did not publish all its interviews of the autopsy witnesses. Many of the 26 interviews, along with other records, were sealed for 50 years, until 2029.

The House Committee claim was difficult to believe. In a report that appears in Volume 18 of the 26 Volumes, Secret Service agent Clinton Hill had written that when he arrived at the morgue after the autopsy, he observed a "wound on the right rear portion of the skull." (November 30, 1963, 18H745)

David Lifton, author of *Best Evidence*, which covers the autopsy in detail, interviewed a number of people present at the autopsy who contradicted the House Committee claim. Autopsy photographer John Stringer told Lifton the wound was "in the occipital." (August 25,

1972 interview reported in *Best Evidence*, page 516)   James Jenkins, a lab technologist, told Lifton the wound was in the "parietal and occipital section on the right side of the head." (September 23, 1979 interview, page 616)   Jerrol Custer, an X-ray technician, said, "he [developed and] returned to the morgue, X-rays showing that the rear of the President's head was blown off." (September 30, 1979 interview, page 620)

In 1993 Congress released to the National Archives the records that were to have been kept sealed until the year 2029. In 1994, Dr. Gary Aguilar, chairman of the Department of Surgery at St. Francis Memorial Hospital in San Francisco, pored through hundreds of the declassified records and discovered that the House Committee had misrepresented what witnesses to the autopsy had said.

Dr. John Ebersole, the radiologist who evaluated the X-rays during the autopsy, told the House Committee that "the back of the head was missing." (HSCA interview with Ebersole, 3/11/78, page 3, National Archives) Jan Rudnicki, an officer and lab technologist for the Bethesda Pathology Department, told an investigator for the House Select Committee on Assassinations that the "back-right quadrant of the head was missing." (JFK Records, File #: 014461, Record #: 1801010510397, National Archives) James Metzler, a hospital corpsman who helped carry the body from the coffin to the autopsy table, recalled a wound in the "right side of the head behind the right ear extending down to the center of the back of the skull." (JFK Records, File #: 014465, Record #: 1801010510401, National Archives) Edward Reed, the technician who took X-rays during the autopsy, said that the head wound "was very large and located in the right hemisphere in the occipital region." (JFK Records, File #: 014463, Record #: 1801010510399, National Archives)

Mortician Tom Robinson said the wound was located "directly behind the back of his head." (JFK Records, File #: 000661, Record #: 1891008910178, National Archives)

Despite the assurances of the Warren Commission and the House Select Committee on Assassinations that all medical discrepancies had been put to rest, to this day the evidence on the nature and location of the President's wounds contradicts the Commission and House Committee's findings.

FATAL SHOT

The Zapruder film grimly depicts the assassination. It shows the President lifting his arms as he reacts to his throat wound, and then seconds later, when he is hit in the head, his skull explodes as he is thrown violently back and to the left. The President's violent backward movement conforms to our intuitive understanding of how a bullet propels an object in the direction the bullet is moving. Nowhere in the Warren Report, or in the hundreds of thousands of pages of testimony and documents compiled by the Commission, was this backward motion even mentioned. It was completely ignored. Instead, the Commission reported that when struck in the head,

> The President fell to the left into Mrs. Kennedy's lap. (WR3)

and concluded:

> No credible evidence suggests that the shots were fired from . . . any place other than the Texas School Book Depository Building. (WR61)

On Saturday, November 23, 1963, CBS correspondent Dan Rather was privately shown the Zapruder film.

The public was not allowed to see the film, so Rather described to his audience what the film showed. Inexplicably, he reported that the President's "head went forward with considerable violence."

On October 2, 1964, *Life* magazine published Zapruder frame 313 which depicted the fatal blow, but failed to publish the frames which showed the President's violent backward movement. The Zapruder film was not shown publicly until a pirated copy was aired twelve years later on ABC in March of 1975.

In 1978, in testimony before the House Select Committee on Assassinations, an Army scientist at the Edgewood Laboratory of the Aberdeen Proving Grounds revealed the results of a test he had performed for the Warren Commission back in 1964. In an attempt to simulate the fatal wound, ten skulls had been shot with the Mannlicher-Carcano rifle. All ten skulls, instead of moving back toward the rifle, "moved in the direction of the bullet." (Testimony of Larry Sturdivan, 1H404; JFK Exhibit F305, National Archives)

House Select Committee on Assassinations Claim

The rapid backward movement of the President at the instant his head exploded does not mean that he was shot from the front. Dr. Luis Alvarez, a Nobel Prize-winning physicist, found through theoretical calculations and experiment that at the impact of the fatal shot a "jet effect," a forward stream of blood and brain matter, propelled the President backward and to the left in the opposite direction. (7HSCA174; "A Physicist Examines the Kennedy Assassination Film," *American Journal of Physics*, September 1976) According to an article in *The Journal of the American Medical Association*, "An object struck in the rear by a high-velocity missile similar to the bullets that hit Kennedy *always falls backward* as a result of the jet-propulsion effect created by tissues exploding out the front." ("JFK's Death—The Plain Truth from the MDs Who Did the Autopsy," *JAMA*, May 27, 1992, page 2803)

Evidence

There was no evidence of a jet effect. A mix of blood and brain matter was propelled in all directions. It shot up into the air. It splattered over Governor Connally and his wife. It splattered over motorcycle officer James Chaney riding to the right rear of the limousine. (Interviewed by Bill Lord, WFAA-TV, November 22, 1963) And it splattered over the left rear of the limousine and hit two trailing motorcycle officers, Bobby Hargis and B. J. Martin, striking their clothes and motorcycles. (6H294; 6H292) Hargis was struck so hard by a piece of skull bone that he said, "I thought at first I might have been hit." (Document 21; *New York Daily News*, November 24, 1963; Zapruder Film)

Mrs. Connally testified, "The third shot that I heard I felt, it felt like spent buckshot falling all over us, and then, of course, I too could see that it was the matter, brain tissue, or whatever, just human matter, all over the car and both of us. . . . after the third shot [Mrs. Kennedy] said, 'They have killed my husband. I have his brains in my hand.'" (4H147-8)

If there had been a jet effect, a stream of blood and brain matter would have exploded to the *right front* of the limousine since the President was thrown to the left rear. (Newton's third law of motion: For every action, there is an equal and opposite reaction.) But instead, a stream of blood and brain matter hit the motorcycle officers, who were behind the President at the *left rear* of the limousine throughout the assassination. (*Zapruder Frames*: Frames 313 to 329)

In the fall of 1988, COMTAL–3M Corporation analyzed a film of the assassination taken by Orville Nix.
Its computer-enhanced version of the Nix film shows
blood and brain matter moving toward the left rear of
the limousine. No forward jet spray was observed.
("Who Murdered JFK?" Jack Anderson, November 22, 1988)

The Zapruder film, combined with the testimony of
the two motorcycle officers who were splattered with
blood, brain and bone matter, is compelling evidence
that the fatal shot was fired from the front. It is impossible for someone to be shot from behind, have his
blood, brain and skull matter propelled to the rear, and
fall backward. What propelled the President backward
was the force imparted by a bullet shot from the front.

SINGLE BULLET THEORY

After viewing the Zapruder film, the Warren Commission was confronted with still another problem. This one it tackled in the strangest of ways. The film depicts in sequence the reactions of President Kennedy shot in the throat, Governor Connally shot in the back, and President Kennedy shot fatally in the head. The Olympic rifle champion at that time, Hubert Hammerer, said he doubted he was capable of duplicating Oswald's three shots using the Mannlicher-Carcano, the alleged assassination weapon. (Reuters, November 26, 1963) In essence, the problem for the Commission was: How could Oswald be a better shot than an Olympic champion?

To compound the problem, another bullet was fired that missed. It hit a curb on Main Street near the railroad overpass, and James Tague, who was standing a few feet away, was struck by a fragment of the bullet that ricocheted off the curb and caused a superficial injury to his face. (Documents 1, 2) This evidence suggests at least four shots were fired, assuming one bullet caused the President's throat and back wounds (as the Commission did), a second bullet caused Governor Connally's wounds (it shattered his fifth rib and right wrist and penetrated his left thigh), a third bullet missed and a fourth bullet caused the fatal wound to

the President's head. Four shots with the Mannlicher-
Carcano in that time span was simply impossible. With
the Commission publicly committed to the theory that
Oswald fired three shots, and with only three spent car-
tridge cases found at the sixth floor window, a fourth shot
meant another assassin.

How did the Commission resolve this problem? Incred-
ibly, it concluded that one bullet struck both President
Kennedy and Governor Connally. Oswald didn't have to
fire four shots after all.

Warren Commission Claim

"Although it is not necessary to any essential findings of the Commission to determine just which shot
hit Governor Connally, there is very persuasive evidence from the experts to indicate that the same bullet
which pierced the President's throat also caused
Governor Connally's wounds." (WR19)

Evidence

The Single Bullet Theory has been attacked on several grounds. But the main problem with it is that the
President's and Governor's wounds do not line up
with a single shot from the sixth floor window according to the Commission's own test.

The Commission claimed that the President had been
hit in the neck between Zapruder frames 210 and 225.
Although the FBI neglected to use the Presidential limousine in its reconstruction of the assassination, it
appears that a bullet striking the President in the neck
would not hit Governor Connally where he was wounded
just below his right armpit. (Documents 4, 22) The
Commission's own test, though flawed, undermined its
Single Bullet Theory.

COMMISSION EXHIBIT 399

The single bullet, Commission Exhibit 399, which was found on a stretcher at Parkland Hospital, was only slightly deformed. In tests conducted by the Warren Commission, a bullet fired through a cadaver's wrist was flattened, while bullets fired into cotton were only slightly distorted. (Document 23) These tests gave rise to the question: How could Commission Exhibit 399 inflict all the wounds to the President and the Governor and look like a bullet fired into cotton?

House Select Committee on Assassinations Claim

When Commission Exhibit 399 struck the Governor's wrist, it was travelling at a reduced velocity since it had first struck the President's neck and the Governor's chest. A bullet striking the Governor's wrist at a reduced velocity would be no more deformed than Commission Exhibit 399. (HSCA Report 45; 7HSCA172)

Evidence

The conclusions reached by the Warren Commission and the House Select Committee on Assassinations were based on conjecture and not experiment. The proper test, which has yet to be performed, would be to line up two cadavers and fire a single bullet through the neck of one and the chest and wrist of the other.

The test that has come the closest to simulating the conditions of the Single Bullet Theory was performed by a staunch defender of the lone assassin theory, Dr. John Lattimer, a urologist at Columbia Presbyterian Medical Center. Animal tissue was used to simulate the President's neck. In place of the Governor's torso was a rib cage. Nothing was used to simulate his back or chest muscles. Radius bones "encased in simulated forearms" were used in place of the Governor's arm. According to Dr. Lattimer, out of approximately 20 attempts, four bullets struck all three objects. A photograph of one of the test bullets appears in Dr. Lattimer's paper reporting the results of his experiments. (*Journal of American College of Surgeons*, May 1994) It was split at the nose in several places and was significantly more deformed than Commission Exhibit 399. I asked Dr. Lattimer if I could examine and photograph this bullet and the other three bullets, as well, and he told me that he had thrown them all away. (Filmed interview of Dr. Lattimer, May 20, 1997)

NEUTRON ACTIVATION ANALYSIS

The Single Bullet Theory is critical to answering the question of how many bullets were fired. If one bullet did not strike both the President and the Governor, then at least three shots must account for all their wounds. Since one shot missed (it ricocheted off a curb, superficially wounding James Tague on the cheek), that means four shots and another assassin. To support the Single Bullet Theory, the House Select Committee on Assassinations engaged Dr. Vincent Guinn, professor of chemistry at the University of California at Irvine, to conduct a neutron activation analysis of Commission Exhibit 399 to see if it matched fragments found in Governor Connally's wrist.

House Select Committee on Assassinations Claim

According to Dr. Guinn, fragments from the same Mannlicher-Carcano bullet have similar, if not identical, levels of antimony which can be measured using neutron activation analysis. He determined that a fragment from Commission Exhibit 399 had 833 ppm (parts per million) of antimony, while a fragment removed from Governor Connally's wrist had 797 ppm, a difference so slight (only 36 ppm) that he concluded that the wrist fragment had come from bullet 399. (1HSCA504; 1HSCA538)

Evidence

In his report commissioned by the House Committee, Guinn described how he tested three bullets, acquired six years earlier independently of the Committee. He took four fragments from each bullet and tested them under neutron activation analysis for traces of antimony. His results, excerpted in the following table, appeared on page 549 of volume 1 of the hearings of the House Select Committee on Assassinations.

Fragment	Bullet A	Bullet B	Bullet C
1	363 ppm	358 ppm	1062 ppm
2	395 ppm	869 ppm	1139 ppm
3	441 ppm	882 ppm	1156 ppm
4	667 ppm	983 ppm	1235 ppm

This table shows that the antimony level in a Mannlicher-Carcano bullet is by no means unique.

Furthermore, it is a scientific and mathematical fact that since the antimony levels of bullet B range from 358 ppm to 983 ppm, bullet B must contain fragments with an antimony level of 833 ppm. Thus, bullet B, which had no connection to the assassination, contains fragments that exactly match the antimony level of the fragment from Commission Exhibit 399 (833 ppm).

The table, which amazingly is from Guinn's own experiments, contradicts his claim that he could distinguish Mannlicher-Carcano bullets from each other. Evidently, in an attempt to please the Committee that hired him, Dr. Guinn put his politics ahead of his science and misrepresented the results of his neutron activation analysis.

The Single Bullet Theory, more appropriately dubbed the Magic Bullet Theory by attorney Mark Lane in his book *Rush to Judgment*, is utterly implausible. As Lane has often quipped, with some hyperbole, "The magic bullet strikes the President in the back of the neck at a downward angle, leaving behind a wound in his back below the shoulder; it rises and exits the President's throat, leaving behind a small neat wound of entrance; then it hangs out there in midair for a second until it observes Governor Connally, makes a sharp right turn and strikes Connally in the back, shatters his fifth rib, exits his chest and shatters his right wrist, makes a left turn and lands in his left thigh bone, and finally, exhausted from its adventures, falls out, wholly intact and only slightly deformed."

EASY SHOT

⟨At the time of the assassination, rifle experts familiar with the Mannlicher-Carcano doubted that anyone could carry out the assassination with that weapon. As the Warren Commission put it:

> ⋆ *Speculation.*— Oswald could not have fired three shots from the Mannlicher-Carcano rifle in [5.6] seconds. (WR645)

In response to this speculation, the Warren Commission claimed "to test the rifle under conditions which simulated those which prevailed during the assassination." (WR193) The Commission's simulation, however, bore little resemblance to the conditions of the assassination.

Although Oswald was classified as a "rather poor shot" in the Marines, the Commission chose three marksmen rated Master, the National Rifle Association's highest ranking, to fire the rifle. (WR191; WR193; 19H18)

Although the Commission claimed Oswald fired from the sixth floor window 60 feet above the ground, it had the Master riflemen fire from a 30-foot tower. (Document 24)

Although the President was a moving target for the assassin, the Commission had the Master riflemen fire at three stationary targets at 175, 240 and 265 feet from the tower. (Document 25)

Although the President was struck in the head and upper back, the three Master riflemen fired at a larger target area that represented the region of a man's body above the waist. (Document 26)

Each Master rifleman fired two series of three shots, for a total of 18 rounds. What happened? Two of the three master riflemen were unable to fire the rifle as quickly as Oswald allegedly did. The best riflemen in the world were 1 to 2 seconds slower than Oswald. These two Master riflemen took from 6.4 to 8.25 seconds, while Oswald supposedly took under 5.6 seconds. (WC193) To accept the Commission's version of what happened, one is forced to believe that two of the best riflemen in the world were slower than Oswald.

Despite this relatively slow pace, they missed the target completely 5 times. Not one of the 18 shots fired by the three expert riflemen struck the head or neck region of the target. What did the Commission conclude this test proved?

> The various tests showed that the Mannlicher-Carcano was an accurate rifle and ... Oswald had the capability to fire three shots, with two hits, within 4.8 to 5.6 seconds. . . . it was an easy shot. (WR195)

The New York Times, in the introduction to its edition of the Warren Report, supported the Commission assessment of the rifle test. The *Times* reported that although Oswald had "no special qualifications as a marksman, . . . demonstrations by a moderately skilled person showed that no genuine difficulty was imposed in duplicating the feat." (*The New York Times/Bantam* edition of the Warren Report, 1964, page xxvii)

Warren Commission Claim

The Italian Mannlicher-Carcano, the assassination weapon, is, "in fact, as accurate as current military weapons." (WR195)

Evidence

Independent rifle experts dismiss this assessment of the weapon. Walter Harold Black Smith, one of the most renowned rifle experts of this century, wrote in 1945 that the Mannlicher-Carcano rifles "are poor military weapons in comparison with United States, British, German or Russian equipment." (*Basic Manual of Military Small Arms*, Third Edition, page 195) *Mechanix Illustrated* claimed the Mannlicher-Carcano "is crudely made, poorly designed, dangerous and inaccurate . . . unhandy, crude, unreliable on repeat shots, has safety design fault." (October 1964)

The Mannlicher-Carcano was designed in 1891 and last manufactured in 1941. Oswald supposedly used a carbine version, with a barrel 9 inches shorter than the original 1891 design, rendering the rifle even more inaccurate.

Warren Commission Claim

"In the Marine Corps he [Oswald] is a good shot, slightly above average, and as compared to the average male . . . throughout the United States, he is an excellent shot." (WR192)

Evidence

The analogy is foolish. Millions of men in this country have never fired a rifle. Compared to them Oswald might have been a great shot. When Oswald entered the marines, he received training in the use of the M-1 rifle. After three weeks he scored low in the sharp-shooter category, which was average for that amount of practice. The last time Oswald fired a rifle in the Marines he shot one point above the minimum qualifying score. One of his friends, Nelson Delgado, remembered "it was a pretty big joke, because he got a lot of 'Maggie's drawers'," which meant not only missing the target but completely missing, as well, a large canvas sheet that held the target. (8H235) Lieutenant Colonel A. G. Folson, Jr. explained to the Warren Commission that Oswald's final score "indicates a rather poor shot." (WR191; 19H18)

CBS News Claim

CBS News reconstructed the assassination with the Mannlicher-Carcano for a 1967 documentary. Eleven marksmen made 37 attempts to fire three shots at a moving target from a 60-foot tower. Out of the 37 attempts to fire three shots, seventeen of those attempts were not counted "because of trouble with the rifle." CBS never revealed what the "trouble" was. "In the 20 attempts [remaining] where time could be recorded, the average was 5.6 seconds." A weapons engineer had three hits in 5.2 seconds; a Maryland state trooper had two out of three hits in slightly less than five seconds; a technician at a ballistics lab had one hit in 4.1 seconds, while another state trooper had one hit in 5.4 seconds. Walter Cronkite, whom a Gallup poll found to be the most trusted man in America, looked in the camera and said, "How fast could Oswald's rifle be fired? . . . It seems reasonable to say that Oswald, under normal circumstances, would take longer [than experts]. But the circumstances were not normal. He was shooting at a President. So our answer is probably fast enough." ("The Warren Report, Part I," *CBS News*, June 25, 1967) "It was an easy shot," said Dan Rather. (Part III, June 27, 1967)

Evidence

CBS divulged only four of the twenty attempts made by the eleven marksmen. Did the other marksmen hit the target at least two out of three times? Presumably, if the seven other marksmen whose scores were not revealed had averaged two out of three hits on the target, CBS would have said so. In a documentary 26 years later, CBS finally disclosed that only four out of the eleven marksmen managed two hits out of three. ("Who Killed JFK? The Final Chapter," *CBS Reports*, November 22, 1993) Clearly, shooting at a moving target with the Mannlicher-Carcano is a difficult task even for experts.

Warren Commission Claim

Oswald would perform trial runs "sighting with the telescopic lens and operating the bolt." Several times he went out for target practice. (WR192) Furthermore, "the use of a four-power scope was a substantial aid to rapid, accurate firing." (WR195) "It requires no training at all to shoot a weapon with a telescopic sight once you know that you must put the crosshairs on the target." (WR190)

Evidence

A telescopic sight won't make you a marksman. Trial runs and a few "target practices" won't make you a marksman either, any more than swinging a racket in your living room will make you a tennis champion. The rifle experts used in the Warren Commission and CBS reconstructions were among the best riflemen in the world. The Commission found that after Oswald left the marines he went hunting only two times with a rifle, and it was never able to establish that he ever practiced shooting at a rifle range. (WR192) To reach the top of any profession requires years of commitment. Oswald never came close to putting in the required time.

Warren Commission Claim

Tests determined that "the defect [in the mounting of Oswald's scope] was one which would have assisted the assassin aiming at a target which was moving away." (WR194)

Evidence

Since the rifle could not be fired accurately with the defect in the mounting, the Warren Commission had the scope's mounting realigned before their marksmanship tests were performed. (3H444)

U.S. News & World Report Claim

The assassination was an easy shot, made even easier because the Presidential limousine came "to almost a standstill" before the fatal shot. (September 6, 1993, page 78)

Evidence

The limousine maintained a speed of over 10 miles per hour before the fatal shot. *U.S. News & World Report's* claim that the limousine came almost to a standstill is easily proved to be a fabrication by examining a witness in the background of the Zapruder film. Mary Moorman, who can be spotted wearing a dark raincoat, moves across the frames of the Zapruder film at a constant rate of speed right up until the fatal shot at frame 313. (*Zapruder Frames*: Frames 290 to 313)

Even the Warren Commission was unwilling to bend the truth here. It reported that the limousine moved down Elm Street at approximately 11 miles per hour. "The car maintained this average speed over a distance of approximately 136 feet immediately preceding the shot which struck the President in the head." (WR49)

THE TIMING OF THE SHOTS

The Zapruder film is more than a photographic record of the assassination; it is a time clock as well. Zapruder's camera ran at 18.3 frames per second. Knowing that makes it possible to determine the time frame of the assassination.

The Commission thought it unlikely that Oswald would have fired before frame 210, because a large oak tree obscured his view of the President from frames 166 to 210, a total of 44 frames or 2.4 seconds. (WR98)

Since the fatal shot to the President's head occurred at Zapruder frame 313, if the President was hit in the neck as early as frame 210, the firing time would have to be 5.6 seconds.

WHICH SHOT MISSED?

The oak tree did not deter the House Select Committee on Assassinations from claiming that Oswald fired and missed the first shot at Zapruder frame 160 which extended Oswald's firing time for the assassination to 8.4 seconds. (HSCA Report 81)

Does the extended firing time of 8.4 seconds allow enough time for an average shooter to aim and fire three shots accurately? Even expert marksmen struggle at this speed. One of the Master riflemen firing at three stationary targets in the Warren Commission's rifle test took 8.25 seconds and hit only two of the three stationary targets. On his second attempt he took 7 seconds but hit only one of the three targets. (3H446) To believe the House Committee's version of the assassination, one must believe Oswald could fire a rifle as well as this master marksman.

The Warren Commission thought it unlikely that the first shot missed because of "the improbability that the same marksman who twice hit a moving target would be so inaccurate on the first and closest of his shots as to miss completely, not only the target, but the large automobile." (WR111) If the assassination were an easy shot, why did the first shot, the easiest of the shots, miss?

Anyone familiar with Dealey Plaza must wonder, if Oswald were the lone assassin, why he did not shoot when the President was in clear view as the limousine rode towards him on Houston Street, or when the limousine slowly made a 120 degree turn at the corner, or when it rode over 100 feet down Elm Street before it passed beneath the oak tree.

The Warren Commission was reluctant to conclude that any of the shots missed, although a shot ricocheted off a curbstone near the overpass, causing a fragment to cut bystander James Tague on the cheek. (Documents 1, 2) Tague testified he felt a sting on his face but was not sure whether it was caused by the second or third shot. (7H555) After a patrolman noticed that Tague had blood on his cheek, a mark on a curb near where Tague was standing was found. Tague said, "There was a mark quite obviously that was a bullet, and it was very fresh." (7H553)

The portion of the curb that contained the bullet mark was not removed by the FBI until August 4, 1964, over eight months after the Commission was formed. When the FBI examined the mark it found traces of lead and antimony. (WR116) This finding was significant since Oswald supposedly used copper-jacketed bullets. The absence of copper raises the possibility of another assassin using different ammunition. The Commission never considered this possibility, but it did concede that "one shot probably missed." (WR117)

According to *U.S. News & World Report* there is a rational account of the assassination that explains how Oswald missed the first shot, and why copper was absent from the bullet mark on the curb. That account, the magazine proclaimed, is found in *Case Closed* by Gerald Posner.

U.S. News & World Report Claim

"Posner now performs the historic office of correcting the mistakes and laying the questions to rest with impressive finality, bringing the total weight of evidence into focus more sharply than anyone has done before." Posner has determined that prior to Zapruder frame 210, Oswald fired the first shot at the President through a large oak tree. "That shot was almost certainly deflected by a branch," which stripped the bullet of its copper jacket. The lead core continued to travel over 400 feet, ricocheting off the curb near the overpass and cutting James Tague on the cheek. (September 6, 1993, pages 91-92)

In a desperate attempt to give Oswald more shooting time, *U. S. News & World Report* embraced a wildly speculative theory that contains its own astounding magic bullet.

It is not unreasonable to speculate, without any supportive evidence, that Oswald somehow refrained from taking an early shot when the Presidential limousine was turning onto Elm Street, and instead, chose to shoot through a tree obstructing his view. But to turn such speculation into evidence to support the lone assassin theory eliminates all pretence of an honest effort to determine the truth.

JIGGLE ANALYSIS

In a bold attempt to prove to a scientific certainty the lone assassin theory, CBS News reported in 1967 the results of their "jiggle analysis" of the Zapruder film. Dr. Luis Alvarez, a physicist at the University of California at Berkeley, related to CBS that it was likely that Abraham Zapruder was not able to hold his camera steady when he heard the shots fired. Consequently, significant blurring would occur after each shot was fired. ("The Warren Report, Part 1," *CBS News*, June 25, 1967)

To determine the maximum number of shots, all one has to do is look for blurs in the film caused by Zapruder jiggling his camera. Of course, blurring could occur by panning errors as Zapruder turned his camera to follow the Presidential limousine. But if only three blurs existed in the film this would be strong evidence that at most three shots were fired.

Dr. Alvarez pointed out that a blur, in reaction to a shot, would not occur immediately. The human nervous system just cannot transmit signals fast enough from the brain to the muscles for that to happen. The neuromuscular reaction takes about a quarter of a second, or approximately five frames of the Zapruder film, to respond to a shot. Thus, since the fatal shot occurred at frame 313, a sequence of blurred images should begin five frames later. And in fact, frames 318 to 322 are blurred.

CBS found two other blurred sequences and concluded only three shots were fired. The first shot (which CBS said missed) occurred at frame 186, and the second shot (the magic bullet) occurred at frame 222.

There was a problem with the jiggle analysis, however, which CBS failed to reveal—CBS and Dr. Alvarez did not agree on where the blurred frames occurred. Dr. Alvarez, in a paper that appeared in the *American Journal of Physics*, thought the blurred frames occurred earlier. He placed the first shot at frame 177 and the second shot at frame 216. (September 1976)

Another problem with the CBS and Alvarez analyses was that the first and second shots were placed too close together. The Warren Commission found that an expert marksman using the Mannlicher-Carcano could not fire two shots in less than 2.3 seconds. (WR97) This translates to less than 42 frames of film, since Zapruder's camera ran at 18.3 frames per second. In the CBS study the first two shots differ by 36 frames (less than 2 seconds) and in Dr. Alvarez' study they differ by 39 frames (2.1 seconds). If either CBS News or Dr. Alvarez were correct, either would have inadvertently proved that Oswald, firing with the Mannlicher-Carcano, was not the lone assassin.

In 1978 the House Select Committee on Assassinations made its foray into jiggle analysis. Its photographic evidence panel determined that the first and second shots were fired at frames 160 and 190. (HSCA Report 83) These two shots would have differed by only 30 frames (1.6 seconds), but the House Committee never explained how a marksman, let alone Oswald, could fire the Mannlicher-Carcano that fast.

Just how many blurs are there in Zapruder's film? Collectively, three different jiggle analyses have concluded that shots were fired at seven different frames: 160, 177, 186, 190, 216, 222 and 313.

In 1993 *U.S. News & World Report* endorsed the House Committee's jiggle analysis as supporting evidence that the first shot was fired at frame 160. Evidently realizing that a second shot fired at frame 190 shatters the lone assassin theory (only 1.6 seconds would separate shots fired at frames 160 and 190), the magazine disagreed with the House Committee on the timing of the second shot and advanced the theory that it occurred instead at frame 224. (September 6, 1993, pages 92-95) An expert marksman would now have enough time to fire two shots in the interval between frames 160 and 224 (3.5 sec); nonetheless, there is a problem with frame 224. If there was a shot at frame 224, then there should be a sequence of blurred frames beginning at frame 229. Frames 228 through 233, however, are among the clearest in the film.

In a program for CBS News on November 22, 1993, Dan Rather reviewed the jiggle analysis CBS conducted twenty-six years before. This time, however, Rather did not reveal which frames were blurred. In a pitiful attempt to give credence to the lone assassin theory, Rather said, "Zapruder slightly jiggled his 8 mm camera three times causing the film to blur." ("Who Killed JFK? The Final Chapter," *CBS News*, November 22, 1993)

GRASSY KNOLL

Many witnesses to the assassination thought the shots came from behind a gently sloping grassy knoll where railroad tracks and a parking lot are located. (Documents 1, 2) Ochus Campbell, Vice President of the Book Depository, who was standing in front of the Book Depository building, said, "I heard shots being fired from a point which I thought was near the railroad tracks located over the viaduct on Elm Street." (Documents 1, 2; 22H638)

Jean Newman, who was standing at the foot of the knoll, told the FBI that "when she realized the reports were shots she immediately turned and looked up the hill to the north toward the parking lot." (22H843)

At the sound of the shots, Dallas deputy sheriffs Harry Weatherford and J. L. Oxford ran across Dealey Plaza. As Weatherford wrote in his report on November 23, "I was running towards the railroad yards where the sound seemed to come from." (19H502)

Paul Landis, Jr., a Secret Service agent standing on the right running board of the car immediately behind the Presidential limousine, stated, "My reaction at this time was that the shots came from somewhere towards the front." (18H759)

Forrest Sorrels, the Secret Service agent in charge of the Dallas Office, was riding in the car in front of the Presidential limousine. He testified, "The noise from the shots sounded like they may have come back up on the terrace there [grassy knoll]." (7H346)

PUFF OF SMOKE

In addition, railroad workers on the overpass saw a puff of smoke rise from the trees in front of a wooden fence at the top of the grassy knoll. (Documents 1, 2) Deputy Sheriff A. D. McCurley wrote in his report on November 22 that "A railroad worker stated to me that he believed the smoke from the bullets came from the vicinity of a stockade [wooden] fence." (19H514)

Railroad worker S. M. Holland, in a Dallas Sheriff affidavit made out the afternoon of the assassination, wrote, "I looked over toward the arcade and trees [the knoll] and saw a puff of smoke come from the trees." (19H480) Later Holland told the Warren Commission, "A puff of smoke came out about 6 or 8 feet above the ground right out from under those trees." (6H243)

The Warren Commission ignored Holland's testimony and never addressed the fact that five other railroad workers claimed to have seen smoke on the knoll at the time of the shots. They were James Simmons and Richard Dodd (both interviewed by Mark Lane in the film *Rush To Judgment*), Austin Miller (19H485), Walter Winborn and Thomas Murphy.

In May of 1966 I spoke with Thomas Murphy and Walter Winborn, who were standing on the overpass at the time of the assassination.

> Galanor. Could you tell me where you thought the shots came from?
>
> Murphy. Yeah, they come from a tree to the left, of my left which is to the immediate right of the site of the assassination.
>
> Galanor. That would be on that grassy hill up there.
>
> Murphy. Yeah, on the hill up there. There are two or three hackberry and elm trees. And I say it come from there.
>
> Galanor. Well, was there anything that led you to believe that the shots came from there?
>
> Murphy. Yeah, smoke.
>
> Galanor. You saw smoke?
>
> Murphy. Sure did.
>
> Galanor. Could you tell me exactly where you saw the smoke?
>
> Murphy. Yeah, in that tree. (May 6, 1966; JFK Records, ARRB 5.1, Galanor, Stewart, National Archives)

Winborn told me he saw

> "smoke that come out from under the trees on the right hand side of the motorcade. . . . It looked like a little haze. Like somebody had shot firecrackers or something like that. Or

somebody had taken a puff off of a cigarette and maybe probably nervous and blowing out smoke. Oh, it looked like it was more than one person that might possibly have exhaled smoke. But it was a haze there. From my general impression it looked like it was at least ten feet long and about, oh, two or three feet wide." (May 5, 1966; JFK Records, ARRB 5.1, Galanor, Stewart, National Archives)

The FBI agents who interviewed Winborn for the Warren Commission, however, did not mention in their report that he had seen smoke on the knoll. (22H833)

> Galanor. Did you tell them about that, that you saw smoke on the grassy knoll?
> Winborn. Oh yes. Oh yes.
> Galanor. They didn't include it in their report.
> Winborn. Well.
> Galanor. Do you have any idea why they didn't?
> Winborn. I don't have any idea. They are specialists in their field, and I'm just an amateur. (May 5, 1966; JFK Records, ARRB 5.1, Galanor, Stewart, National Archives)

Thirty years after the assassination, *U.S. News & World Report* sought to settle, once and for all, the claim that witnesses saw a puff of smoke. Using excerpts from Gerald Posner's *Case Closed*, the magazine dismissed witness accounts of seeing a puff of smoke on the knoll as having no probative value.

U.S. News & World Report Claim

Railroad workers on the overpass could not have seen a puff of smoke from rifle fire on the knoll, "because modern ammunition is smokeless, it seldom creates even a wisp of smoke." (September 6, 1993, page 86)

Evidence

You can easily disprove this claim by visiting your local rifle range. Just watch people shoot. You will see puffs of smoke all over the place. Even the House Select Committee on Assassinations conceded that "modern weapons do in fact emit smoke when fired." (HSCA Report 606; 7HSCA373)

U.S. News & World Report Claim

"James Simmons said [to the FBI] he thought the shots came from the School Book Depository and that he saw 'exhaust fumes' from the embankment." (September 6, 1993, page 86)

Evidence

This is indeed what two FBI agents claim Simmons said to them in March of 1964. (22H833) This FBI report, however, is a fabrication. One of *U.S. News & World Report's* main flaws, which it shares with other major news media and the Warren Commission, is its unquestioning reliance on hearsay reports of FBI agents. Many witnesses contradicted what was in their FBI reports, and Simmons was one of them. Simmons told Mark Lane in a filmed interview, "It sounded like it came from the left and in front of us towards the wooden fence. And there was a puff of smoke that came underneath the trees on the embankment. . . . It was right directly in front of the wooden fence." Simmons told the FBI agents when they visited him that he had seen a puff of smoke on the knoll. Evidently, they chose to hand in a false report instead. (The film *Rush to Judgment*)

U.S. News & World Report Claim

"Austin Miller thought the smoke he saw was 'steam'. . . It is likely that any smoke seen was in fact steam. A steam pipe ran along the wooden fence near the edge of the triple underpass." (September 6, 1993, page 86)

Evidence

Not quite. *U. S. News & World Report* did not accurately represent what Austin Miller said. In a sworn statement to the Dallas Sheriff's Department on November 22, Austin Miller said, "I saw something which I thought was smoke or steam coming from a group of trees north of Elm off the railroad tracks." (19H485) When he was questioned four and a half months later by Commission counsel David Belin, he was not asked one question about the smoke or steam he observed. The steam pipe referred to in *U.S. News & World Report* can be seen in the film *Rush to Judgment*. It is over 100 feet away from the point on the knoll where smoke was observed by the six railroad workers. (Document 2) No one reported smoke or steam at the location of the steam pipe. If a steam pipe had been the cause of smoke at the site of the steam pipe or on the grassy knoll, one would expect the steam or smoke to have been seen again. No such sightings occurred.

U.S. News & World Report Claim

"Clemon Johnson [another railroad worker] saw white smoke but told the FBI that it 'came from a motorcycle abandoned near the spot by a Dallas policeman.'"

Evidence

The railroad workers saw a puff of smoke right after they heard the last shot. There was no motorcycle on the knoll at that time, as photographs taken after the assassination by a witness, Wilma Bond, clearly show. (Document 27)

AN FBI AGENT'S ANALYSIS

Former FBI agent James Hosty, who was assigned to investigate Oswald prior to the assassination, has recently felt compelled to use his forensic talent to disprove the claim that witnesses saw a puff of smoke. Hosty, in his memoirs, *Assignment: Oswald*, writes, "Of all the people standing in Dealey Plaza, only one described seeing a puff of smoke near the tree line along the grassy knoll at approximately the same time the first shot fired and missed. That's it. Nothing more. Over the years, many conspiracy theorists have taken this 'puff' and either extrapolated a second gunman out of it or have distorted the evidence to prove there was a second gunman." (*Assignment: Oswald*, Arcade: New York, 1996, page 252)

SECRET AGENT

Police officer Joe Marshall Smith was stationed at the intersection of Elm and Houston when he heard shots which he thought were coming from bushes near the overpass. (22H600) When he arrived at the parking lot behind the knoll he approached a man walking among the parked cars, and as Smith later testified,

> Smith. I pulled my pistol from my holster, and I thought, this is silly, I don't know who I am looking for, and I put it

> back. Just as I did, he showed me that he
> was a Secret Service agent [by holding up
> his identification badge].
>   Liebeler. Did you accost this man?
>   Smith. Well, he saw me coming with my
> pistol and right away he showed me who
> he was. (7H535)

At least two other witnesses reported they were
denied access to the top of the knoll. Gordon Arnold
claimed that he was asked to leave the parking lot area
behind the knoll by a "Secret Service agent" prior to the
assassination. (Trask, Richard, *Pictures of the Pain*) Malcolm
Summers, who ran up the knoll after the assassination,
said, "We were stopped by a man in a suit, and he had
an overcoat over his arm and I saw a gun under that
overcoat. His comment was, 'don't you all come up
here any further you could get shot.'" ("Who Murdered
JFK?", Jack Anderson, November 22, 1988)

According to the House Select Committee on
Assassinations, however, there were no Secret Service
agents on the knoll after the assassination. Chief counsel for the House Committee reported, "A careful
examination of where all of the Secret Service agents
were that day, and their duty assignments, indicates
that no Secret Service agent was in that area [the
knoll]." (5HSCA589)

Who was the "Secret Service agent" that Officer
Smith encountered and what was he doing there?
Why did the Warren Commission not even attempt to
locate and question him? And why did he not come
forward to report what he saw on the grassy knoll?

WITNESSES

Staff photographer for the *Dallas Times Herald* Bob Jackson was riding in a press car, eight cars behind the President's in the motorcade. After Jackson heard the last shot, he looked up at the Book Depository and saw the barrel of a rifle recede into the sixth floor window and yelled, "Look up in the window! There's the rifle!" (WR65) In the car with Jackson were Malcolm Couch, a television newsreel cameraman, and Tom Dillard, chief photographer of *The Dallas Morning News*. Couch turned quickly enough to see about a foot of the rifle barrel brought into the window. Dillard grabbed his camera and as the press car passed the Book Depository he took a photograph of the upper floors. (WR66) Dillard did not react fast enough to catch the barrel of the rifle, but his photograph and the testimony of Jackson and Couch are substantial evidence that the sixth floor window of the Book Depository was the source of at least one of the shots fired.

Over six hundred people witnessed the assassination of President Kennedy. The Warren Commission never compiled a list of witnesses to the assassination, nor did it give any credence to eyewitness accounts that shots came from the grassy knoll.

In 1978 the House Select Committee on Assassinations had Dr. David Green, a consultant retained by Bolt Beranek and Newman, a firm specializing in acoustic research, analyze the accounts of the witnesses that "were available to the Warren Commission." Dr. Green was chairman of Harvard's psychology department and an expert on what he called "psychoacoustics." (HSCA Report 87)

The eyewitness accounts analyzed by the House Committee and Dr. Green were from testimony taken by the Warren Commission and from FBI reports published in the 26 Volumes of Hearings and Exhibits that accompanied the Warren Report.

ANALYSIS OF 178 WITNESSES

House Select Committee on Assassinations Claim

"The statements of 178 persons who were in Dealey Plaza, all of whom were available to the Warren Commission, were analyzed": 21 (11%) thought the shots came from the grassy knoll area, 49 (27%) thought the shots came from the Book Depository, 78 (44%) could not tell where the shots came from, and 30 (17%) believed the shots originated elsewhere. (HSCA Report 87)

Evidence

The Committee was somewhat flustered by these statistics and concluded that "while recognizing the substantial number of people who reported shots originating from the knoll the Committee also believed . . . it would be unwise to place substantial reliance upon it." (HSCA Report 87) The main problem with the House Select Committee's analysis is that it did not provide a list of the 178 witnesses and their statements regarding the origin of the shots. Therefore, the authenticity of its work could not be substantiated. Which witnesses, according to the Committee, thought the shots came from the knoll; which thought they "originated elsewhere"? Without this information the Committee's analysis could not be verified.

ANALYTICAL FLAWS

In his report to the Committee Dr. Green revealed that a House Committee investigator had determined that "692 people were present in the Plaza during the assassination." (8HSCA139) It appears that neither Dr. Green nor the Committee made a serious attempt to reach more than a few of the 692 witnesses. As Dr. Green stated in his report, "The sheer size of the sample [178 witnesses] makes it difficult to believe that a sizeable selection bias was present." (8HSCA139) The Warren Commission, however, received reports from 57 Dallas Police, Deputy Sheriffs and Secret Service agents present in Dealey Plaza during the assassination. Thus, the sample size of 178 witnesses was comprised of a disproportionate number of government agents who traditionally tend to identify with the government's case. Hence, the Committee's selection process did not come close to producing a random sample. Therefore, Dr. Green's claim that an accurate statistical analysis could be performed was false.

FOUR ISSUES

In analyzing the witness accounts, a sedulous investigator would consider various problems which were never addressed by Dr. Green or the House Committee.

1 — ACCOMMODATING WITNESSES

One delicate issue to confront is the truthfulness of some of the witnesses. Jesse Curry, the Dallas chief of police, told reporters on November 23 that he "could tell from the sound of the three shots that they had come from the book company's building near down-town Dallas." (*The New York Times*, November 24, 1963) Curry was driving the lead car of the motorcade, the car in front of the Presidential limousine. However, when confronted with the transcript of the police radio trans-missions, Curry admitted that just after the shots were fired, he broadcast over his car radio: "Get a man on top of that triple underpass and see what happened up there." (23H913; 4H161)

Some witnesses eagerly bend the truth; others need a little prodding. House Speaker Tip O'Neill revealed in his autobiography that five years after the assassination

> I was surprised to hear [Presidential aide Kenneth] O'Donnell say that he was sure he had heard two shots that came from behind the fence.
> "That's not what you told the Warren Commission," I said.
> "You're right," he replied. "I told the FBI what I had heard, but they said it couldn't have happened that way and that I must have been imagining things. So I testified the way they wanted me to. I just didn't want to stir up any more pain and trouble for the family." (*Man of the House*, page 178)

Some witnesses, even members of the press, bend the truth because they tend to identify with the government's case. Associated Press photographer James Altgens told the Commission he thought the shots came from behind the President. (7H517) But on November 22, he sent out over an AP dispatch, "At first I thought the shots came from the opposite side of the street [i.e., the knoll]. I ran over there to see if I could get some pictures." (Document 28)

2 — DEFICIENT INTERROGATIONS

A second issue to consider is: How diligent was the Warren Commission in obtaining the witnesses' accounts? Many interviews do not report where the witness thought the shots originated. The FBI interviewed 83 witnesses for the Commission. Out of those 83 reports, 42 do not mention the witness's opinion on the origin of the shots. (See *216 Witnesses* Appendix)

Although the FBI interviewed Orville Nix twice, absent in the agents' reports is the direction from which he thought the shots came. In a film interview, Nix told Mark Lane that, although he now believes the shots came from the Book Depository, at the time of the shooting "I thought it came from a fence between the Book Depository and the railroad track." (The film *Rush to Judgment*)

Dallas Police officer Clyde Haygood told Commission counsel David Belin that when the shots were fired he ran to the railroad yard behind the knoll. Yet Belin never asked him to give his opinion on the origin of the shots. (6H298)

Another Dallas Police officer, Seymour Weitzman, reported on November 22, "I ran in a northwest direction and scaled a fence towards where we thought the shots came from." (24H228) When he appeared before Commission counsel Joseph Ball four months later, he was not asked to give his opinion on the source of the shots.

3 — ERRONEOUS REPORTS

A third issue to consider is: Did FBI and Secret Service agents submit erroneous reports to the Warren Commission? In an FBI report to the Warren Commission, two FBI agents, Trettis and Robertson, related that railroad track supervisor Richard Dodd "did not know where the shots came from." (22H835) Many witnesses contradicted what was in their FBI reports, and Dodd was one of them. Dodd told Mark Lane in a filmed interview that he told federal agents that "the shots, the smoke came from behind the hedge on the north side of the plaza." (The film *Rush to Judgment*)

Secret Service agent Glen Bennett, riding in the rear seat of the car behind the President's, claimed to have written in his notes the day of the assassination that "I saw a shot that hit the Boss about four inches down from the right shoulder. A second shot followed immediately and hit the right rear high of the Boss's head." (24H542) Although the Warren Commission never interviewed Bennett, it concluded, "Substantial weight may be given Bennett's observations . . . his notes indicate that he recorded what he saw and heard at 5:30 p.m., November 22, 1963, on the airplane en route back to Washington, prior to the autopsy, when it was not yet known that the President had been hit in the back." (WR111) A more demanding Commission would have examined photographs of the assassination to see if Bennett was at least looking at the President when the shots were fired. Alas, photographs taken by witnesses show Bennett looking off to his right toward the knoll long after he claimed to have turned to look toward the President. (Document 29)

4 — WITNESSES NOT CALLED

The final issue to confront is that the Commission never called most of the witnesses. Aurelia Alonzo, Anne Donaldson and Mary Woodward, reporters for *The Dallas Morning News*, were standing near the cement arch on the grassy knoll watching the motorcade. Woodward wrote for her paper the next day: "Suddenly there was a horrible, ear-shattering noise coming from behind us and a little to the right [the knoll]." (*The Dallas Morning News*, November 23, 1963) Alonzo and Donaldson were never interviewed by the Warren Commission or the FBI. Would they have testified that they thought the shots came from the grassy knoll? Most likely, since Alonzo told a *Texas Observer* reporter that although she might have been confused, "The sound [of the shots] seemed to be coming from above our heads. I wasn't sure. We looked up behind us. There are some trees, there are some cement structures [the knoll]." (*Texas Observer*, Ronnie Dugger, December 13, 1963)

Ed Johnson, a reporter for the *Fort Worth Star-Telegram*, was riding in the motorcade. He was never interviewed by any government agency. But he wrote for his paper the next day, "Some of us saw little puffs of white smoke that seemed to hit the grassy area in the esplanade that divides Dallas' main downtown streets." (*Fort Worth Star-Telegram*, November 23, 1963)

Nowhere in Dr. Green's report, and nowhere in the 12 volumes of hearings and reports of the House Select Committee, will one find the slightest indication that Dr. Green or the House Committee ever considered these four issues in analyzing witness accounts. The House Select Committee's analysis is incomplete and misleading and therefore, another analysis of witness accounts is required to draw any valid conclusions as to the origin of the shots.

ANALYSIS OF 216 WITNESSES

My reading of the testimony and statements of 216 witnesses available to the Warren Commission reveals that 70, or 32%, were not asked where they thought the shots came from. Of the remaining 146 witnesses, 54 (37%) thought the shots came from the grassy knoll area; 46 (32%) thought the shots came from the Book Depository or close by; 35 (24%) could not tell where the shots came from; 6 (4%) believed the shots came from both the knoll and the Book Depository; only 5 (3%) believed the shots originated elsewhere. (See *216 Witnessess* Appendix)

How is one to explain the difference between these figures and the figures of the House Committee? This discrepancy can be partially explained by Dr. Green's tendency to misrepresent where witnesses placed the origin of the shots. He pointed out that Josiah Thompson, author of *Six Seconds in Dallas*, claimed that Abraham Zapruder, who was standing on the knoll taking his famous 8 millimeter film, thought the shots came from behind him. (Documents 1, 2) Dr. Green sought to discredit Thompson's assessment by citing Zapruder's sworn testimony before the Warren Commission:

> Liebeler. But you didn't form any opinion at that time as to what direction the shots did come from actually?
> Zapruder. No.

And thus, Dr. Green and the House Committee placed Zapruder in the "Could Not Tell" category. (8HSCA141)

A less biased investigator would have noticed that Zapruder sought to please Commission counsel when he answered "No" to Liebeler's leading question. Earlier in the questioning when Liebeler had asked, "Did you have any impression as to the direction from which these shots came?" Zapruder responded, "No, I also thought it came from back of me [grassy knoll]." (7H572) A more thorough investigator would have found the Secret Service Report that stated, "According to Mr. Zapruder, the position of the assassin was behind Mr. Zapruder." (Warren Commission Document 87, Folder 1, Secret Service Control No. 66, National Archives)

DECLASSIFIED ANALYSIS

In 1993 the House Select Committee's records were declassifed and stored in the National Archives, but the Committee's analysis of the witnesses' accounts was not among them. In 1997 I acquired from Bolt Beranek and Newman Dr. Green's analysis of the accounts of 178 witnesses. It finally became possible to see how the Committee represented witness accounts of the origin of the shots. (JFK Records, ARRB File 5.1, Galanor, Stewart, National Archives)

Many witnesses pointed to the railroad tracks behind the knoll and the overpass next to the knoll as the source of the shots. Dallas Deputy Sheriff Harold Elkins stated, "I immediately ran to the area from which it sounded like the shots had been fired. This is an area between the railroads and the Texas School Book Depository which is east of the railroads." (19H540) Ronald Fischer told the Warren Commission that "They [shots] appeared to be coming from just west of the School Book Depository Building. There were some railroad tracks and there were some railroad cars back in there." (6H195) Peggy Hawkins told the FBI that "she immediately recognized [the shots] as firearm shots and not as fireworks and had the impression that they came from the direction of the railroad yards adjacent to the TSBD Building." (Warren Commission Document 897) Dolores Kounas and Avery Davis, who were standing in front of the Book Depository, both told the FBI that the shots appeared to come from west of the Book Depository. Kounas said, "I did not look up at the building as I had thought the shots came from a westerly direction in the vicinity of the viaduct." (22H659) Davis said, "I did not know from which direction the shots had come, but thought they were from the direction of the viaduct which crosses Elm Street west from where I was standing." (22H642) Neither Elkins, Fischer, Hawkins, Kounas nor Davis explicitly mention the knoll, but clearly they were referring to that region of Dealey Plaza. Nevertheless, the House Committee placed these five witnesses in the "Elsewhere" category. (JFK Records, ARRB File 5.1, Galanor, Stewart, National Archives)

Jane Berry, Wesley Frazier and William Shelley were also standing in front of the Book Depository. The FBI reported that Berry said that "It sounded as if it had been fired from a position west of where she was standing." (Warren Commission Document 5) Frazier told the Warren Commission, "Well to be frank with you I thought it come from down there, you know, where that underpass is. There is a series, quite a few number of them railroad tracks running together and from where I was standing it sounded like it was coming from down the railroad tracks there." (2H234) Shelley, when asked by Warren Commission counsel, "What seemed to be the direction or source of the sound?" said, "Sounded like it came from the West." (6H329) The

House Committee placed these three witnesses in the "Could Not Tell" category. (JFK Records, ARRB File 5.1, Galanor, Stewart, National Archives)

Victoria Adams and Dorothy Garner viewed the motorcade from fourth floor windows of the Book Depository. Adams testified before the Warren Commission that "It seemed as if it [shots] came from the right below rather than from the left above." (6H388) Garner told the FBI, "I thought at the time the shots or reports came from a point to the west of the building." (22H648) Despite their accounts the Committee counted Adams and Gardner as witnesses who thought the shots came from the Book Depository. (JFK Records, ARRB File 5.1, Galanor, Stewart, National Archives)

ECHOES

The House Committee was clearly troubled by its own statistics, and it sought to explain why so many witnesses "erroneously" thought the shots came from the region of the grassy knoll. Several witnesses had tried to reconcile their recollection of events with the Government's version that all the shots came from the sixth floor window of the Book Depository Building. When asked by Commission counsel why he ran to the railroad yard behind the grassy knoll, Deputy Sheriff Luke Mooney said, "from the echo of the shots, we thought they came from that direction." (3H283) The Committee also took this tack.

House Select Committee on Assassinations Claim

Many witnesses were confused about the origin of the shots because Dealey Plaza is an echo chamber. Shots fired from the Book Depository sound as if they came from the grassy knoll. (8HSCA137)

Evidence

Echoes are caused by sound bouncing off large, hard surfaces, as anyone who has ever shouted in a canyon knows. There are no buildings on the knoll or overpass that would have reflected sound back to confuse witnesses in Dealey Plaza. Beyond the knoll the terrain is flat with railroad tracks, while the knoll is covered with grass, shrubs and trees that absorb sound. If there were echoes, they would have been caused by the sound of rifle fire from the knoll echoing off the Book Depository.

ANALYTICAL TRAPS

It seems that Dr. Green and the House Select Committee on Assassinations, like the Warren Commission, fell into that most dangerous of analytical traps. In analyzing witness accounts they assumed, like the Warren Commission, that all the shots came from the Book Depository. That was their assumption when they started, and that assumption conditioned the way they looked at almost every piece of evidence. Evidence that supported their point of view was credible, and evidence that did not support that point of view was not credible or not relevant.

In Dr. Green's report to the Committee he observed that when the Mannlicher-Carcano was test-fired from the knoll, the rifle shots were "very very loud." He was "unable to understand how they could have been described as a firecracker or backfire," by many of the witnesses. (8HSCA148) Thus, for him "it was hard to believe a rifle was fired from the knoll. Such a shot would be extremely loud, even if silenced, and it would be hard to imagine anyone in the vicinity of the knoll missing such an event." (8HSCA150) Dr. Green was so committed to the assumption that all the shots were fired with a Mannlicher-Carcano that it was evidently impossible for him to acknowledge that a quieter modern weapon fired from the knoll might have sounded like firecrackers or backfire to the witnesses.

It was the Warren Commission's obligation, which fifteen years later became the House Select Committee's responsibility, to conduct an exhaustive and unbiased investigation. The Commission interviewed only 78 out of over 600 witnesses, often botching the interview by failing to solicit the witness's view on the origin of the shots. The House Select Committee's investigation was equally deficient. At most, it purported only to have surveyed the eyewitness accounts published by the Warren Commission, never revealing the names of the witnesses surveyed or their accounts of the assassination. It misrepresented witness accounts to the assassination and covered up critical information, as did the Warren Commission.

BACKYARD PHOTOGRAPHS

In February 1964, a number of mainstream newspapers and magazines began publishing a photograph of Oswald posing with a rifle and Communist newspapers in the backyard of his house. The photograph appeared on the cover of *Life* magazine on February 21, three months after the assassination, with a caption identifying Oswald with the rifle he used to assassinate President Kennedy. (Document 30) Almost immediately, however, the authenticity of the photograph was questioned. The photograph clearly had been tampered with. All rifles have an indentation in the stock so that you can reach the trigger to fire it. Yet the stock of the rifle on the cover of *Life* magazine is straight with no indentation, while the stock of the Mannlicher-Carcano is indented. (Document 31)

Doubts about the photograph's authenticity increased when several variations were published. The photograph appeared in *The New York Times* with the telescopic sight missing from the rifle. (February 19, 1964) It appeared in *Newsweek* with the telescopic sight removed and metal added near the bolt. (Document 32) Nevertheless, the Warren Commission "concluded that the rifle shown in [the original of] these pictures is the same rifle which was found on the sixth floor of the Depository Building on November 22, 1963." (WR125)

House Select Committee on Assassinations Claim

Twenty-two of the nation's leading photography experts examined the backyard photos utilizing sophisticated photographic techniques to determine their validity. Calvin McCamy, head of the photographic panel, said, "We found no evidence whatsoever of any kind of faking in these photographs." (2HSCA418)

Evidence

A distinguished independent photographic expert differed with the House Committee's findings. Detective Superintendent Malcolm Thompson of England, head of the Police Forensic Science Laboratory Identification Bureau of Scotland Yard, went on record that the photographs were forgeries.

The British Broadcasting Company relayed to the House Committee an interview with Thompson in which he pointed out discrepancies between the shadows in the photograph. (6HSCA221) It had been pointed out to the Warren Commission that the shadow from Oswald's nose falls in the middle of his mouth, indicating the sun was directly overhead, but the shadow of Oswald's body angles slightly off to his right, indicating the sun was slightly to his left. (Document 30) Thompson told the BBC that "one can only conclude that Oswald's head has been stuck onto a chin not being Oswald's chin. Then, to cover-up the montage, retouching has been done. . . . They are fakes." (*The Plot to Kill the President*, BBC, 1978) A comparison of the *Life* photograph with a Dallas police mug shot of Oswald taken on November 23 shows the chins are entirely different, which indicates that the head was superimposed at the chin where a line is visible. (Document 33)

The House Committee related that Thompson deferred to the conclusions of their photographic panel, but at the same time they also acknowledged that he "reserved his opinion" on the difference between the chins in the two photographs.

Of course, photographs can be deceiving and misrepresent reality. We have all seen pictures of people we know that do not look like them. Photography experts for the House Committee pointed out that Marina Oswald remembered taking the backyard photographs, and that there are other photographs of Oswald where his chin appears square. But other aspects of this photograph remain puzzling.

When the photograph of Oswald holding the rifle was shown to him during his interrogation he said, as FBI and Secret Service agents later reported, it was "possible that the Police Department had superimposed this part of the photograph [his head] over the body of someone else," and "at the proper time he would show that the photographs were false." (FBI Agent Bookhout, WR625; SS Inspector Kelly, WR628)

Warren Commission Claim

"A photography expert with the FBI photographed [an FBI agent with] the rifle used in the assassination attempting to duplicate the position of the rifle and the lighting" of the backyard photograph. (WR125) With the FBI photography expert able to duplicate the shadow disparity, the Commission concluded "the photograph was not a composite of two different photographs and Oswald's face had not been superimposed on another body." (WR127)

Evidence

The duplicate photograph was not published in the Warren Report. It was buried, instead, in the 26 Volumes. On page 522 of Volume 17 one finds the photograph the

Commission claimed duplicated the lighting of the backyard photograph. Alas, the head of the FBI agent was removed. (Document 34) If the FBI were able to duplicate the shadows of the backyard photograph, would it have removed the head? In admitting the duplicate photograph into evidence, Commission counsel asked the FBI photography expert, Mr Shaneyfelt, "I see the head of the individual in the photograph is blacked out. Can you explain the reason for that?" Mr. Shaneyfelt replied, "I blanked out the head because it was one of the employees of the FBI, and I felt it was desirable to blank out the head since it was not pertinent."

In 1966 *The London Times* decided to conduct its own test on this question of the shadow disparity. Its photographers were unable to duplicate the lighting of the backyard photograph. (Document 35) *The London Times's* test shows that when the shadow of the nose falls straight down, the shadow of the body is behind. When the shadow of the nose veers off to the right, so does the shadow of the body.

Where the FBI and *The London Times* failed, CBS apparently succeeded. In a 1967 documentary, CBS produced a photograph taken by Lawrence Schiller with the same shadow configurations of the backyard photograph. ("The Warren Report, Part I," *CBS News*, June 25, 1967) Schiller refused to grant permission for his photograph to appear in this book.

MICHAEL PAINE'S STORY

If it could be shown that Oswald possessed the photograph before the assassination, then it would have to be genuine. Michael Paine was the owner of the home where Marina Oswald lived for two months prior to the assassination and where Oswald stayed on weekends. When Paine was interviewed by CBS in 1993 he related, "I went one afternoon to pick him [Oswald] up, went up stairs, and I think the first thing he did, practically, was pick up this photograph of himself, 8 by 10, holding his rifle there and some papers. I was a little startled, I suppose he was looking for a big revolution, and he'd join the revolution with his gun." ("Who Killed JFK?, The Final Chapter", *CBS News*, November 22, 1993) Paine had kept this information to himself for over thirty years. If he were telling the truth, then he lied under oath to the Warren Commission when he said, "I didn't know prior to the assassination, we didn't know he had a rifle." (2H418)

On the same CBS program Michael Paine completely undermined his credibility when he said, "At the police station when I saw him [Oswald] later on that night [November 22] he was proud of what he had done. He thought he would be recognized now as somebody who did something." There are two problems with Paine's account. First: He told the Warren Commission he never saw or spoke to Oswald at the police station. (2H430) Second: Oswald never displayed any pride in killing the President. In fact, he said emphatically that he didn't shoot anyone.

CBS anchor Dan Rather, who hosted the program, did not challenge Paine on the conflict between his testimony before the Warren Commission and what he told CBS. Instead, Rather remarked, "There isn't a reporter in the world, including this one, who wouldn't love to uncover something, anything, that would decisively reverse or positively confirm the current weight of the evidence."

STILL ANOTHER PHOTOGRAPH

More doubts about the photograph's authenticity surfaced in February, 1992, when the Dallas City Council, in response to Oliver Stone's movie *JFK*, released all documents from the Dallas Police Department files on the assassination. In those files was discovered a photograph of a white silhouette figure of the type used in a darkroom in one of the steps to combine photographic images. (Document 36) This photograph suggests that an attempt was made to frame Oswald, confirming his suspicion that it was "possible that the Police Department had superimposed this part of the photograph over the body of someone else."

Is the backyard photograph of Oswald a fake, or was it taken by Marina Oswald as she testified, and then subsequently doctored? The record is not conclusive. The record does reveal, however, the mindset of the Warren Commission, which was willing to accept questionable evidence as authentic so long as it supported the lone assassin theory.

CASE AGAINST OSWALD

The case against Oswald developed by the Dallas Police, the FBI and the Warren Commission, if left unchallenged, appears overwhelming.

PARAFFIN TEST

When the case against Oswald was first being developed by the Dallas Police and the FBI over the weekend of the assassination, the most important evidence presented was the result of the paraffin test given to Oswald the afternoon of November 22. On Saturday, November 23, Dallas Police Chief Jesse Curry told reporters that the paraffin test used by his department for detecting gun powder traces was positive, proving that Oswald fired a gun. (24H764) Curry's statement was reported in every major newspaper and magazine in America. It was quickly broadcast over radio and television and was the most important piece of evidence, at least from an emotional standpoint, establishing Oswald as an assassin.

In summing up the case against Oswald, *The New York Times* reported:

> Gordon Shanklin, FBI agent in charge at Dallas, said today that . . . a paraffin test,

used to determine whether a person has fired a weapon recently, was administered to Oswald shortly after he was apprehended Friday, one hour after the assassination. It showed that particles of gunpowder from a weapon, probably a rifle, remained on Oswald's cheek and hands. (*The New York Times*, Fred Powledge, November 25, 1963)

There were two problems with this report. First, the paraffin test does not test for gunpowder. It tests for nitrates which are found in gunpowder that escapes from the breech when the rifle is fired. In theory, if someone who is right-handed had recently fired a rifle, then paraffin casts of his left hand and cheek would have no traces of nitrates (negative) while casts of his right hand and cheek would (positive). The test, however, can never substantiate that someone has fired a weapon, because nitrates are found in other substances such as cigarettes and lighted matches, soap, cosmetics, toothpaste, paint, and other common household goods. (WR561) For this reason police departments have abandoned the paraffin test as unreliable.

The second problem was that the paraffin casts of both of Oswald's hands showed nitrates, and the cast of his right cheek was negative. (WR560) The result was consistent with the possibility that Oswald did not fire a rifle. When the Dallas Police conducted the paraffin test, they were assuming it was a valid test. Although the test did not establish Oswald's innocence, the police should have reported that it was consistent with Oswald's innocence. Instead, the Dallas Police distorted the result of the test, and the FBI and the major media repeatedly misrepresented what the test could determine.

The lesson here is that scientific tests depend on the integrity of the people who conduct and interpret them. Independent and unbiased experts must be allowed access to the evidence. Indeed, American jurisprudence guarantees adversarial examination of the evidence since unbiased judgments are so difficult to insure.

The Warren Commission reported that the results of Oswald's paraffin test were negative. But neither the Dallas Police nor any major newspaper, magazine or television network retracted the reports, heard over and over again the weekend of the assassination, that the paraffin test proved Oswald had fired a rifle.

Thirty years after the assassination, *Newsweek* was still misrepresenting the results of the paraffin test by reporting that "the FBI lab identified traces of nitrate on Oswald's hands" as if the finding were indicative of guilt. (November 22, 1993, page 76)

PALMPRINT

Early on Saturday morning, November 23, the Dallas Police, after examining the Mannlicher-Carcano for fingerprints, sent it off to the FBI headquarters in Washington. The FBI fingerprint expert, Sebastian Latona, was unable to find a single identifiable print on the rifle. When asked by the Warren Commission why no identifiable prints were found on the rifle, Latona responded:

> First of all the weapon itself is a cheap one. ... A cheap old weapon. The wood is to the point where it won't take a good print to begin with hardly. The metal isn't of the best, and not readily susceptible to a latent print. (4H29)

Indeed, the fingerprints of Dallas Police Captain Will Fritz, who first picked up the rifle, worked the bolt and ejected a live round, were not found on the rifle. (WR122, 4H23)

Seven days passed before the FBI was informed by the Dallas Police that there had been a recognizable palmprint on the barrel. The reason the FBI did not discover it, according to the Warren Commission, was that Lieutenant J. C. Day of the Dallas Police, using Scotch tape, had lifted the palmprint completely off the rifle without leaving a trace before it was sent to the FBI. (WR123) Lieutenant Day, however, told the FBI that after he made the lift he "could still see this palmprint on the underside of the barrel of the gun." (26H832)

Another of Day's actions added to the mystery. Day did not adhere to the routine procedure of photographing the palmprint before lifting it, although he did photograph two unidentifiable prints he found on the trigger guard. Inexplicably, when Day sent the rifle to the FBI, he included the photographs of the useless unidentifiable prints but kept the lifted palmprint in Dallas. (WR123)

Lieutenant Day's examination of the rifle disturbed the Commission's general counsel, J. Lee Rankin, enough to prompt an FBI memorandum that stated,

> Rankin advised, because of the circumstances that now exist, there was a serious question in the minds of the Commission as to whether or not the palm[print] impression that has been obtained from the Dallas Police Department is a legitimate latent palm impression removed from the rifle barrel or whether it was obtained from some other

source and that for this reason this matter needs to be resolved. (FBI memorandum from Rosen to Belmont, August 28, 1964, page 3; Released by FBI on January 18, 1978, National Archives)

At Rankin's request, the FBI reexamined the palm-print. This time the FBI found that the palmprint was lifted from the rifle since "the adhesive material bearing the print also bore impressions of the same irregularities that appeared on the barrel of the rifle." (WR123)

Subsequently, the Commission sought to resolve the question of the legitimacy of the palmprint by asking Lieutenant Day to sign a statement verifying that he had lifted it. Day refused. (26H829)

Thirty years later, public television's *Frontline* documentary reported that a fingerprint expert had succeeded where so many had failed. The two unidentifiable fingerprints on the trigger guard in the photographs that Day took can now be identified as Oswald's. In 1963, less than 24 hours after the assassination, Latona had used gray fingerprint powder and "highlighting, sidelighting, every type of lighting that we could conceivably think of." (4H21) He concluded "that the latent prints which were there were of no value." (WR123) To accept *Frontline's* conclusion we must believe photographs of the fingerprints are clearer than the real prints were to Latona in the FBI laboratory thirty years before. ("Who was Lee Harvey Oswald?" November, 1963)

MAIL ORDER RIFLE

The day after the assassination the FBI announced that Oswald ordered a Mannlicher-Carcano rifle through the mail using the alias A. Hidell. Inexplicably, he had bought a cheap Italian rifle that could be traced through the mail when he could have anonymously bought an accurate weapon at any number of gun shops in Dallas.

The rifle was supposedly shipped to Oswald's post office box in March of 1963. If Oswald expected to receive a rifle addressed to Hidell, he would have authorized Hidell to receive mail through his post office box. But the Warren Commission said it was not known whether Hidell was entitled to receive mail through Oswald's post office box, because

> in accordance with postal regulations, the portion of the application which lists names of persons, other than the applicant, entitled to receive mail was thrown away after the box was closed on May 14, 1963. (WR121)

This claim was not correct, since the Post Office regulations required that

> the third portion of box rental applications, identifying persons other than the applicant authorized to receive mail, must be retained for two years after the box is closed. (Documents 37, 38)

The possibility exists that a postal worker unintentionally destroyed the application form, but the Commission's inaccurate representation of evidence linking the Mannlicher-Carcano to Oswald severely called into question the integrity of its investigation.

The post office also required by law that anyone receiving a rifle through the mail must sign a receipt which must be retained for four years. (Document 38) This post office receipt was missing as well.

When Oswald was arrested on November 22, he had recently opened a post office box. This time the box was not closed, but again that part of the application authorizing people to receive mail was mysteriously missing. Since Oswald had been arrested and charged with murder, the person or persons who destroyed the application engaged in the destruction of evidence.

STAR WITNESS

The Warren Commission's star witness was a forty-five-year-old steamfitter, Howard Brennan. According to the Commission, Brennan "made a positive identification of Oswald as being the person at the window." (WR250) He was the only witness to claim he saw Oswald fire a rifle from the sixth floor window. Brennan was sitting on a retaining wall on Elm Street, opposite the Book Depository, when he heard the shots. (Document 39) According to the Warren Commission, "after hearing the first shot . . . Brennan glanced up at the window." (WR144) Brennan testified that he saw a man in the window aiming for his last shot. "It appeared to me he was standing up and resting against the left window sill." (WR144) "Brennan saw the man fire the last shot and disappear from the window." (WR144)

One problem with Brennan's testimony was that if the assassin had been standing as he fired, he would have fired through glass, for the window was only partially open. However, none of the glass panes were broken, and the Commission was forced to contradict its own witness: "Although Brennan testified that the man in the window was standing when he fired the shot, most probably he was either sitting or kneeling." (WR144)

Although Brennan saw a man kneeling who he thought was standing, he testified that he was able to estimate his height to be 5 feet 10 inches tall, which was within an inch of Oswald's height. The Commission resolved this question as follows: "Brennan could have seen enough of a kneeling or squatting person to estimate his height." (WR145)

On the night of the assassination, Brennan viewed Oswald in a police lineup and was unable to make an identification of Oswald as the man he saw in the window. (WR145; 3H148; 24H203) Several days later Brennan was visited by a Secret Service agent who asked him, "You said you couldn't make a positive identification. . . . Did you do that for security reasons personally, or couldn't you?" (3H148) Did Brennan take the hint? When the FBI visited him about two weeks later on December 17, Brennan told them that "he was sure that the person firing the rifle was Oswald." (WR145) He could have identified Oswald at the lineup after all, but as he later told the Warren Commission, "I still believe it was a Communist activity. . . . and if it got to be a known fact that I was an eyewitness, my family or I, either one, might not be safe." (3H148)

However, when the FBI reinterviewed Brennan on January 7, 1964, he said he could no longer make a positive identification of Oswald as the man he saw in the window. (WR145) Then in his appearance before the Warren Commission he once again changed his story and identified Oswald. The Warren Commission never challenged Brennan during his testimony. At a trial would Brennan's "positive identification" have held up under cross-examination?

MARINA OSWALD

The Mannlicher-Carcano was found hidden among some boxes on the sixth floor of the Book Depository fifty-two minutes after the assassination. One of the ways the Warren Commission tried to connect this rifle to Oswald was through his wife, Marina. When the Secret Service questioned Marina a few days after the assassination, she could not identify the rifle. She said that "she did not know that rifles with [telescopic] scopes existed." Marina also explained that "Lee expressed to her that Kennedy was a good President" and that she believed her husband was innocent. (Secret Service Interview, Warren Commission Document 344, pages 23 and 43, National Archives)

Nevertheless, after being held incommunicado for nine weeks by the Secret Service and receiving $132,000 in advances for the rights to her story, Marina emerged before the Warren Commission as its most damaging witness against Oswald. She identified the Mannlicher-Carcano as "the fateful rifle of Lee Oswald" and testified she believed her husband had killed the President. (WR128; 1H492)

Twenty-five years later on a TV documentary by columnist Jack Anderson, Marina reverted to her original belief that Oswald was innocent. When Anderson asked her, "Was he the kind of a man who could have wanted to go down in history as the killer of a president?" she replied, "I never could buy idea that Lee did not like or want to kill President Kennedy. Everything that I learned about President Kennedy was good through Lee."

Marina no longer claimed that the rifle shown to her by the Warren Commission was Oswald's. When Anderson asked her, "Do you think it's possible someone could have persuaded him to leave it [rifle] or planted a rifle?" Marina replied, "Somebody could plant the rifle." She went on to say, "I had been used by the Warren Commission . . . that investigated so dishonestly sometime to make Lee a guilty party. . . . I was very easy mold at the time. I was very young, immature and naive." She now believes that "he [Oswald] was working for the government, and he was just simply infiltrating groups. He was doing what he had been told to do. . . . I'm not saying that Lee was involved in the plot. He was implicated in the plot." ("Who Murdered JFK?", Jack Anderson, November 22, 1988)

Marina's testimony before the Warren Commission contained so many obvious contradictions that a senior counsel for the Commission, Norman Redlich, complained to the general counsel J. Lee Rankin that "Marina Oswald has repeatedly lied to the [Secret] Service, the FBI, and this Commission." (Memorandum from Redlich to Rankin, February 28, 1964, National Archives; 11HSCA126)

An example of Marina's ability to spin an incredible story is an incident she originally related to her business manager. Maria said Oswald had told her one morning that he was going to kill Richard Nixon. She thwarted the murder by locking Owald in the bathroom all day. (1H482-3) Eventually, it must have occurred to her that it was impossible to restrain someone in this way for she later testified that she prevented him from leaving by physically restraining him. "We actually struggled for several minutes and then he quieted down." (5H389)

Unfortunately, the Warren Commission declined to challenge Marina on the veracity of her testimony, even when she contradicted herself. Over the years she has reversed herself so often on matters of dispute that it seems senseless to give any credibility to her testimony or to anything she now has to say.

MOTIVE

The Warren Commission did "not make any definitive determination of Oswald's motives." (WR22) Although it claimed "many factors were undoubtedly involved in Oswald's motivation for the assassination," (WR423) it did not hesitate to hazard a guess. "He sought for himself a place in history—a role as the 'great man' who would be recognized as having been in advance of his times." (WR423) This explanation conveniently overlooks the fact that Oswald did not proclaim his guilt to the world, and instead maintained he was innocent.

SECURING FACTS AND TRUTH

The Warren Commission claimed to have "functioned neither as a court presiding over an adversary proceeding nor as a prosecutor determined to prove a case, but as a factfinding agency committed to the ascertainment of the truth." (WRxiv) Absent, however, from the Warren Commission's investigation was any procedure for challenging the evidence.

At the outset of the Commission's hearings Marguerite Oswald, Oswald's mother, retained attorney Mark Lane to represent her son's interests before the Commission. The Commission denied her request to have Lane represent her son and, in an effort to appear objective, appointed instead the President of the American Bar Association.

> In fairness to the alleged assassin and his family, the Commission on February 25, 1964, requested Walter E. Craig, president of the American Bar Association, to participate

in the investigation and to advise the Commission whether in his opinion the proceed-
ings conformed to the basic principles of
American justice. Mr Craig accepted this
assignment and participated fully and without limitation. (WRxiv)

Craig, however, attended only two of the 51 hearings
of the Commission. The record shows that Craig did
not call one witness for questioning, did not cross-
examine one witness, and did not examine or challenge
any of the physical evidence.

Mark Lane observed at the time that even the Nazi
war criminal, Martin Bormann, was given the benefit of
defense counsel when he was tried *in absentia* at
Nuremberg after World War II. With the Warren
Commission, there was no right to a trial. There was no
right to the presumption of innocence. There was no
right to counsel. There was no right to be confronted by
the evidence against oneself. There was no right to
cross-examine that evidence. There was no right to present a defence of one's own.

In that manner, essential safeguards for securing the
truth were denied, and the evidence went unchallenged, rendering it worthless.

TIME LINES

Oswald was interrogated by the FBI, Secret Service and Dallas Police for 12 hours while he was held in custody. What he said would have been important to any investigation attempting to determine what took place on November 22. These agencies, however, told the Warren Commission that no recordings were ever made of anything Oswald ever said. No stenographic record was made, no notes were taken. The only records that exist are memoranda prepared by investigators "setting forth their recollection of the questioning of Oswald and his responses." (WR598) Although the lack of any kind of verbatim record of Oswald's interrogation hampers any effort to determine where Oswald was at the time of the assassination, an encounter Oswald had with a police officer challenges the Commission's finding that Oswald was on the sixth floor of the Book Depository Building.

The Warren Commission concluded that within 90 seconds of the assassination Oswald was seen in the Book Depository lunchroom by police officer Marion Baker and by Roy Truly, the manager of the Book Depository Building. Within seconds of the shooting, Officer Baker jumped off his motorcycle, ran to the building and asked Truly to show him the way to the roof. (Baker can be seen running into the Depository in a film taken seconds after the assassination by newsreel cameraman Malcolm Couch.)

Baker had his gun drawn when he reached the second floor, and he stopped at the door of the lunchroom and shouted, "Come here," to Oswald. Oswald turned and walked toward Baker. Baker asked Truly, "Do you know this man, does he work here?" Truly replied, "Yes." Baker let Oswald go, and he and Truly continued to run up the stairs to the roof. (WR152)

The Commission claimed Oswald could have descended from the sixth floor window to the lunch-room by the time Baker and Truly arrived, although after several reenactments by Baker and by a Secret Service agent stand-in for Oswald, the Commission admitted it was a close call. (WR152) However, the initial news accounts said that Oswald was drinking a Coke when Baker saw him. This seemingly minor fact raised the question: If Oswald had fired a rifle from the sixth floor window, could he have reached the lunchroom in time to operate a Coke machine and drink some soda before Officer Baker arrived?

In a signed statement written under FBI supervision ten months after the assassination, Officer Baker wrote, "I saw a man [Oswald] standing in the lunchroom drink-ing a Coke."

Supporting Baker's initial observation was a report by Police Captain Will Fritz written after Oswald's murder. He wrote, "I asked Oswald where he was when the police officer stopped him. He said he was on the second floor drinking a Coca-Cola when the officer came in." (WR600)

Although Baker's recollection coincides with Oswald's even on his choice of beverage, inexplicably,

Baker crossed out "drinking a Coke" in his report.
(Document 40; 26H679)

For the time lines of Oswald and Officer Baker to
intersect, Oswald would have had to jog across the
entire sixth floor zigzagging around piles of boxes, hide
the rifle between boxes, descend the stairs to the second
floor, enter the lunchroom, operate a soda machine and
drink some Coke within 90 seconds. Was this possible?
Perhaps. But, once again, the Commission's handling of
the evidence severely undermined the integrity of its
investigation and the veracity of its conclusions.

OSWALD

Although Oswald's life was filled with the intrigue and mystery that one would expect of a secret agent, there is still no solid evidence that he worked secretly for any U. S. intelligence agency. His life contained, however, a series of inexplicable events and encounters that undermine the view that he was acting entirely on his own.

Oswald's favorite program on TV when he was a teenager was *I Led Three Lives*. The show's opening described the hero as an "average citizen, high level member of the Communist Party, and counterspy for the Federal Bureau of Investigation." Acting as if he were inspired by the show to become a counterspy, Oswald started reading communist literature and committed to memory the Marine Corps manual. In October, 1956, at the age of seventeen, he enlisted for a three-year stint in the Marines. (WR681)

MARINES

After basic training, Oswald was sent to Atsugi Naval Air Base in Japan, where super-secret missions of the CIA U-2 spy plane were launched. Although the Warren Commission said he was an avowed Marxist, he was given security clearance to function as a radar operator.

He ostensibly started learning Russian on his own, and later at El Toro Air Base in California he was given the Marine Corps proficiency test in Russian which he failed. At El Toro he openly professed Marxist philosophy and started playing Russian songs so loudly that they were heard outside the barracks. He called his fellow Marines "comrades" and hailed Soviet Communism as the best system in the world. (WR686)

RUSSIA

After leaving the Marines in September of 1959, Oswald traveled to Russia. That October he entered the U. S. Embassy in Moscow, handed over his passport and announced his intention to defect and divulge "classified" material on radar to the Soviets. (5H301) Instead of arresting him on the spot, the Embassy staff allowed him to leave, presumably to divulge military secrets to the Russians.

The Embassy did, however, cable Washington of Oswald's intent. (18H115) Immediately, as Oswald's former commander, John Donovan, told the Warren Commission, the Marine Corps changed all its secret radio and radar frequencies, tactical call signs and its authentication code for entering and exiting the Air Defense Identification Zone. (8H297)

With the fall of the Soviet Union and the opening up of the KGB files, we now know that Oswald's threat to reveal secret information to the Soviets was never carried out, raising further suspicions that his plan to defect was not genuine. In fact, the KGB never thought he was a genuine defector and spied on him for the entire time he was there, going so far as to bug his home and listen in on his most intimate conversations with his wife, Marina. (Norman Mailer, *Oswald's Tale*, Random House)

While in the Soviet Union Oswald lived in Minsk where he worked in a radio factory. Within a year he became disenchanted with Soviet life and wrote to the U. S. Embassy that he wanted to return to America. As it turned out, he had not defected after all. He never signed the papers required to formally renounce his American citizenship, although he had threatened to give away state secrets, a treasonable offense. He was given back his passport and received a loan for travel expenses. With Marina and their baby girl, he returned to America in June 1962. The CIA claimed that they never debriefed Oswald when he arrived in New York, although thousands of tourists were debriefed that year.

TEXAS

Oswald continued to profess Marxism and wrote many friendly letters to communist organizations, but he never attempted to make friends or acquaintances with even one leftist. He and Marina circulated among anticommunist Russian emigres in Fort Worth and Dallas. George De Mohrenschildt, a wealthy Russian baron and oil geologist, became his closest friend. De Mohrenschildt had been suspected of working for the CIA, but no hard evidence has emerged to support this suspicion. Thirty years older than Oswald, De Mohrenschildt became the primary influence over him, arranged a place for Oswald's family to live and helped him search for work. Despite De Mohrenschildt's efforts, Oswald was unable to hold a job for more than a few months at a time.

NEW ORLEANS

In the spring of 1963 Oswald moved to New Orleans and obtained a job, only to be dismissed two months later because of inefficiency and inattention to his work. He attempted to form a chapter of the pro-Castro *Fair Play for Cuba Committee* but was unable to recruit a single member. He handed out leaflets for the Committee stamped with the address "544 Camp St." which was the building where rabid anticommunist and former FBI agent Guy Bannister had a detective agency.

In August Oswald approached Carlos Bringuier, a delegate of an anti-Castro Cuban group. Oswald offered to train Cubans to fight against Castro and gave Bringuier his Marine Corps guidebook. A few days later Bringuier discovered Oswald handing out Fair Play for Cuba leaflets. Bringuier called Oswald a communist pretending to be a friend of the Cuban movement. A scuffle ensued, and they were both arrested. Oswald spent the night in jail, and the next day before his release he asked to see an FBI agent. A local radio station arranged a debate between Oswald and Bringuier which took place toward the end of August.

MEXICO

According to the Warren Commission, in September Oswald traveled to Mexico City with the intention of returning to Russia by way of Cuba. Both the Cuban and Russian embassies denied him visas. Although the CIA had continuous photographic surveillance on both embassies, it was unable to produce for the Warren Commission a single photograph of Oswald entering or leaving either embassy. When Oswald was refused a visa, he got into a heated argument with the Cuban

Consul which ended when the Consul told him that people like Oswald were harming the Cuban Revolution.

DALLAS

Rebuffed by both embassies, Oswald returned to Dallas. He had not worked since July, and he did not work again until October 16 when he was hired to fill book orders at the Texas School Book Depository.

QUESTIONS

Why was an avowed communist in the Marines sent to a secret air base where super-secret U-2 planes were launched? Why was a Marxist in the Marines given a proficiency test in Russian? Why did Embassy officials in Moscow fail to arrest a former Marine threatening to divulge military secrets? How did the CIA fail to debrief a former defector to the Soviet Union? How could a communist living in Texas manage to have only right-wing acquaintances?

Husband and father. Loner and loser. Marxist and Marine. Defector or spy? Agitator or informant? Assassin or patsy? In the end, the inscrutable lives of Lee Harvey Oswald, with all their contradictions and mystery, outnumbered the three lives led by his childhood FBI hero.

JACK RUBY

When Jack Ruby murdered Oswald in the basement of a Dallas jail, he denied our nation the chance to hear from Oswald in a court of law on the question of his guilt or innocence. Although Oswald had proclaimed his innocence, he also said he was a patsy, never elaborating. To even the most naive observer, Ruby became the most important witness on the question: Was there a conspiracy to assassinate President Kennedy?

One of the first issues the Warren Commission should have resolved was when to question Ruby. We can gauge how seriously the Commission was willing to investigate the possibility of a conspiracy by how much time passed before it questioned Ruby. Did two days pass? Two weeks? Two months? It took the Commission over six months before finally questioning Ruby on June 7, 1964. Ruby, in fact, had asked to testify two months earlier. When Ruby finally testified he said, "Well, it is too bad, Chief Warren, that you didn't get me to your headquarters six months ago." (5H192) Is there any reasonable explanation for this delay by the Commission?

WARREN QUESTIONS RUBY

When the Commission finally got around to interviewing Ruby in the Dallas County Jail, he repeatedly asked Earl Warren, "Is there any way to get me to Washington?" (5H190) Warren told Ruby, "I don't know of any," although later in the questioning he admitted to Ruby, "We have the power to subpoena witnesses to Washington if we want to do it." (5H196) Ruby continued to implore Warren to take him to Washington. "Unless you get me to Washington, you can't get a fair shake out of me. If you understand my way of talking, you have got to bring me to Washington to get the [lie detector] tests." (5H191)

In his testimony to the Commission Ruby said he was "as innocent regarding any conspiracy as any of you gentlemen in the room." (5H204) When Warren asked Ruby, "Did you know Lee Harvey Oswald prior to this shooting?" Ruby answered, "That is why I want to take the lie detector test [in Washington]. Just saying no isn't sufficient." (5H196)

Ruby pleaded, "My life is in danger here," and went on to say, "Chairman Warren, if you felt that your life was in danger at the moment, how would you feel? Wouldn't you be reluctant to go on speaking, even though you request me to do so?" Instead of reassuring Ruby that he could speak freely without fear of harm, Warren said, "I think I might have some reluctance if I were in your position; yes, I think I would. I think I would figure it out very carefully as to whether it would endanger me or not. If you think that anything that I am doing or anything that I am asking you is endangering you in any way, shape, or form, I want you to feel absolutely free to say that the interview is over." (5H196)

An investigation committed to determining the truth would have accommodated a witness of Ruby's importance if there was the slightest chance of securing information on his role in a conspiracy. Ruby repeatedly voiced fear for his life and said, "I want to tell the truth, and I can't tell it here." (5H194)

RUBY AND ORGANIZED CRIME

The Warren Commission claimed to have investigated whether Ruby was connected to organized criminal activity. The Commission related, "Virtually all of Ruby's . . . friends stated he had no close connection with organized crime." (WR790) The Commission neglected to tell its readers, however, that many of these friends were connected with organized crime. In fact, one of them, Lenny Patrick, was known as a notorious Syndicate killer. (U.S. Senate, Organized Crime and Narcotics Report, page 37) Patrick told the FBI, "No matter how much you investigate, you'll never learn nothing, as he [Ruby] had nothing to do with nothing." (22H318)

David Scheim, author of *Contract on America*, uncovered an FBI report stored in the National Archives that describes Ruby's close association with Dallas Mafia boss Joseph Civello. The first two paragraphs of this report appear as Commission Exhibit 1536 in the 26 Volumes of evidence. (23H27) The remaining three paragraphs describing Ruby's ties to the Dallas Mafia boss Joseph Civello, however, were omitted. (*Contract on America*, pages 174, 175) Nonetheless, the Commission concluded, "There is no creditable evidence that Jack Ruby was active in the criminal underworld." (WR663)

FBI INFORMANT

Although the Commission denied speculations that "Oswald was an informant of either the FBI or the CIA," (WR660) it did not deny that Ruby had ties with these agencies. Perhaps that was because the head of the FBI, J. Edgar Hoover, sent a letter to the Warren Commission on June 9, 1964, stating that Jack Ruby was an informant for the FBI in 1959.

> Jack Ruby was contacted by Special Agent Charles W. Flynn of the Dallas Office on March 11, 1959, in view of his position as a night club operator who might have knowledge of the criminal element in Dallas. The purpose of this contact was to determine whether or not Ruby did have such knowledge, and if so, if he would be willing to furnish information to this Bureau. Ruby was advised of the FBI's jurisdiction in criminal matters, and he expressed a willingness to furnish information. (Document 41, Letter from FBI Director J. Edgar Hoover, National Archives)

The letter (Warren Commission Document 1052) was never mentioned in the Warren Report or published in the 26 volumes. It was buried in the National Archives where, years later, it was obtained through the Freedom of Information Act.

When Hoover testified before the Warren Commission, he was not asked about Ruby's role as an FBI informant. Apparently, a decision was made to conceal the Hoover letter and Ruby's involvement with the FBI. With this deception, the Commission attempted to quash rumors of Ruby's involvement in a conspiracy.

AUTOPSY X-RAYS

In late October, 1993, less than a month before the thirtieth anniversary of the assassination, radiation oncologist and physicist Dr. David Mantik, from the Eisenhower Memorial Hospital in Rancho Mirage, California, examined the autopsy X-rays stored in the National Archives.

When Dr. Mantik first saw the X-rays he was immediately struck by how extremely white the rear portion of the skull appeared. (Document 42) He expected to see the normal range of white to black that is evident in an X-ray taken of President Kennedy during his lifetime. (Document 43) In an X-ray the whiter regions represent dense tissue, and the darker regions represent less dense tissue. Never in his medical career had Dr. Mantik seen X-rays that looked this white. (Document 42)

For four days he conducted optical densitometry tests on the X-rays, a technique that has been available for many years but had never been applied to study the autopsy X-rays. This technique measures the transmission of ordinary light through selected points of an X-ray. In a normal X-ray, the back of the skull would transmit no more than four times as much light as the front. What he found was astonishing.

The region in the back of the head on the autopsy X-rays transmitted a thousand times more light than the dark region in the front. A transmission of ten times more light might be explained by some variance in human tissue he was unaware of, but a factor of a thousand was inexplicable. Stranger still, the petrous bone that surrounds the inner ear—the densest bone in the body—registered on the X-rays as having essentially the same density as the region at the back of the head. Dr. Mantik was forced to conclude that the autopsy X-rays of President Kennedy's head had been altered. They were composites. The original autopsy X-rays had been rephotographed with a radio-dense patch superimposed over the rear portion of the head, the region precisely where the Parkland doctors had seen a large gaping wound.

In his lab at Eisenhower Memorial Hospital Dr. Mantik photographed X-rays of radio-dense patches superimposed over X-rays to see if he could get similar results. It was surprisingly simple. In the course of just a few minutes, he was able to produce altered X-rays with optical densities like those in the National Archives. ("Optical Density Measurements of the JFK Autopsy X-rays and a New Observation Based on the Chest X-ray" by David Mantik, *Assassination Science*, edited by James Fetzer. Chicago: Catfeet Press, 1998.)

Furthermore, while at the Archives Dr. Mantik noticed that a frontal X-ray showed a metal object which was 6.5 mm in diameter, the same diameter as bullets used for the Mannlicher-Carcano rifle. (Document 44; "JFK Assassination: Cause for Doubt," by David Mantik, *Assassination Science*) However, the autopsy pathologists never mentioned this 6.5 mm circular object in the autopsy report, or in their notes, or in their testimony before the Warren Commission. During the autopsy, X-rays had been taken

DEATH OF THE
LONE ASSASSIN THEORY

When Dr. Mantik returned to Eisenhower Memorial Hospital after examining the autopsy X-rays, he took a cross-sectional CAT scan at the neck level of a patient with upper chest and neck dimensions the same as President Kennedy's. On this CAT scan he drew in the back and throat wounds of the President and connected them with a straight line. (Document 45) Clearly, any bullet along this path would have shattered the spine. But the autopsy pathologists observed and the X-rays confirmed no major trauma to the President's spine had occurred. Thus, a bullet entering the President's back could not have exited his throat. With one simple stroke Dr. Mantik had scientifically disproved the lone assassin theory.

The accumulated evidence indicates that at least four shots were fired: One shot struck the President in the throat, a second shot hit Governor Connally, a third shot ricocheted off a curb and grazed bystander James Tague, and a fourth shot struck the President in the head.

CONSPIRACY

As legally defined, a conspiracy is at least two people acting in concert to commit a crime. The Warren Commission concluded that "No credible evidence suggests that the shots were fired from . . . any place other than the Texas School Book Depository Building." (WR61) Yet its own evidence, found in its 26 Volumes and in the National Archives, suggests that the shots were fired from at least two directions.

EVIDENCE OF A CONSPIRACY

Grassy Knoll
Witnesses heard shots fired from the Book Depository Building and from the grassy knoll. Witnesses ran to the knoll thinking the shots came from there.

Smoke
Six railroad workers and at least one reporter saw a puff of smoke on the knoll.

Rifle Barrel
Two photographers, riding in the motorcade, saw the barrel of a rifle recede from the sixth floor window after the last shot.

Sniper's Nest

A sniper's nest was discovered on the sixth floor of the Book Depository Building, where a rifle and three cartridges were found.

Entrance Wound

Parkland doctors saw an entrance wound in the President's throat.

Back and Throat Wound

The President's back wound was lower than his throat wound. The path through the two wounds does not project upward to the Book Depository.

Head Wounds

The Warren Commission's placement of the President's head wounds does not line up with a shot from the Depository. Instead, the path through the wounds rises from back to front.

Magic Bullet

The Warren Commission's magic bullet could not have entered the back of the neck of the President and exit his throat since his spine was not shattered.

Four Shots

At least four shots were fired: One shot (from the knoll) struck the President in the throat, a second shot (from the Depository) hit Governor Connally, a third shot (from the Depository) ricocheted off a curb and grazed a bystander, and a fourth shot (from the knoll) struck the President in the head.

Backward Body Snap

The President was thrown violently backward to the left rear of the car when he was shot in the head, while two motorcycle officers riding behind and to the left of the President were splattered with his blood and brain matter.

Marksmanship

The majority of rifle experts who participated in the marksmanship tests by the Warren Commission and *CBS News* were unable to duplicate the marksmanship required of the alleged assassin.

None of this evidence, in part or in total, even suggested to the Warren Commission a conspiracy to assassinate the President.

This willingness to ignore evidence is the spirit in which the mainstream media have covered the assassination. In tones reminiscent of overzealous prosecutors, so confident of their arguments, so disdainful of the questions that have been raised, the mainstream media will make any argument, no matter how fatuous or fabricated, to convince us that it is irresponsible and foolish to believe a conspiracy took place.

The editors of *The New York Times* once dismissed the evidence of a conspiracy by proposing what might be called a "coincidence theory." They suggested that if there were a shot from the grassy knoll, perhaps "two independent assassins pulled their triggers in the self-same second." (January 7, 1979)

In spurning evidence of a conspiracy, the news media will often reprove as politically immature those Americans who suspect that politicians conspire to conceal misdeeds. Recent history, however, from Vietnam to Watergate to the Iran-Contra scandal, has given the most innocent among us reason to be skeptical. To hear the media version of the Kennedy assassination is to descend into a world understood from only the most naive perspective of how people behave and how governments work.

COVER-UP

At the start of the Warren Commission's hearings on February 3, 1964, Earl Warren disclosed that the Commission "might not release all of the facts [regarding the assassination] in our lifetime," and added, "I mean that seriously." The next day he told reporters he was just being "a little facetious," but his original statement has unfortunately proved to be accurate. (*New York Post*, February 5, 1964)

About a week or two before President Kennedy was assassinated, Oswald wrote a letter to the FBI which he personally delivered to their office in Dallas. On November 24, shortly after Oswald was murdered, the letter was destroyed by FBI agents. (HSCA Report 185)

In March of 1964, autopsy pathologist Commander Humes testified before the Warren Commission that back on Sunday, November 24, 1963 he had "destroyed by burning certain preliminary draft notes" relating to the autopsy, as well as a draft of the autopsy report. (Document 46; 2H372-4)

In 1978 the House Select Committee on Assassinations discovered that the Army had kept a file on Oswald that it had concealed from the Warren Commission. When the Committee requested the file from the Pentagon they were told that the files had been "destroyed routinely" in 1973. (HSCA Report 224)

Besides the documents published in the 26 Volumes in 1964, thousands of documents were stored in the National Archives. Many of these documents were classified "top secret." They were to remain inaccessible for 75 years, not to be examined by anyone until September, 2039.

In 1992 in response to Oliver Stone's film *JFK*, Congress passed the John F. Kennedy Assassination Records Collection Act, requiring "expeditious disclosure" of all documents related to the assassination. Over the span of four years from 1995 to 1998, sixty thousand records totaling over four hundred thousand pages were released.

Despite the release of suppressed records, a question persists: How many more documents, besides those in the Pentagon, have been "destroyed routinely"?

EVIDENCE OF A COVER-UP

When the Warren Report appeared, it was hailed by the press as "the most massive, detailed and convincing piece of detective work ever undertaken, unmatched in the annals of fact finding," which proved to a certainty that Oswald was the lone assassin. (*The New York Times*, November 28, 1964)

Over the last four decades the mainstream media have acted as an extension of the Warren Commission, misrepresenting evidence countless times to argue that Oswald was the lone assassin. The evidence of a cover-up by the Warren Commission and the mainstream media is extensive:

Evidence Suppressed

Many of the Warren Commission documents that were placed in the National Archives were ordered suppressed until the year 2039. Since the John F. Kennedy Records Collection Act passed in 1992, most of these records have been declassified.

Evidence Fabricated

Instead of introducing into evidence the autopsy X-rays and photographs, the Warren Commission accepted in their place three drawings that did not accurately represent the President's wounds. Two weeks after the assassination *Life* magazine fabricated a story to explain how Oswald could shoot the President in the throat.

Evidence Distorted

Over a period of 14 years the government presented four different versions of the President's wounds.

Evidence Misrepresented

The Warren Commission claimed its goatskin test showed entrance and exit wounds are alike, when in fact they are not. The Commission claimed that three of the best riflemen in the world could emulate Oswald's alleged marksmanship when in fact two of them could not.

Evidence Altered

The head of an FBI agent was removed from a photograph in an attempt to prove that a photograph of Oswald was genuine.

Evidence Doctored

Optical densitometry tests indicate that the autopsy X-rays had been tampered with to hide a large wound in the back of the President's head.

Evidence Falsified

FBI agents handed over to the Commission false reports on where witnesses thought the shots were fired.

Evidence Ignored

The Warren Commission ignored at least seven witnesses who saw puffs of smoke on the grassy knoll. The Commission failed to comment on the President's violent backward movement when he was fatally struck in the head. It never examined the autopsy X-rays.

Evidence Concealed

Life magazine failed to publish the Zapruder frames (314 to 320) that show the President's backward motion at the fatal head shot. The Zapruder film was not shown to American citizens until 12 years after the assassination. The Warren Commission concealed the fact that Jack Ruby was an FBI informant.

Evidence Manufactured

The House Select Committee on Assassinations falsely claimed that neutron activation analysis tests were able to match magic bullet 399 with fragments found in Governor Connally's wrist.

Evidence Omitted

The Warren Commission omitted paragraphs of an FBI report that described Ruby's connection to the Dallas Mafia boss.

Evidence Neglected

The Warren Commission waited over six months to question Ruby about his involvement in a possible conspiracy. The Warren Commission did not attempt to identify the "Secret Service agent" who a Dallas Officer encountered on the knoll.

Evidence Invented

The House Select Committee on Assassinations falsely claimed the President was leaning forward when he was shot to explain why the back wound was anatomically lower than the throat wound.

Evidence Destroyed

A letter Oswald wrote to the FBI was destroyed by FBI agents after the assassination. The chief pathologist burned his notes taken at the President's autopsy and a draft of the autopsy report. Nine years after the assassination Army Intelligence destroyed its secret file on Oswald.

Evidence Contrived

Dan Rather told the nation on the weekend of the assassination that President Kennedy fell forward when he was struck in the head.

From the perspective of today's world, it appears that the Warren Commission's case against Oswald as the lone assassin would have crumbled instantly had the news media sought the truth, relentlessly questioning the Government's version of what happened.

Supreme Court Justice Hugo Black set forth the importance of the media in a democracy when he wrote, "In the First Amendment the Founding Fathers gave the free press the protection it must have to fulfill its essential role in our democracy. The press was to serve the governed, not the governors. The Government's power to censor the press was abolished so that the press would remain forever free to censure the Government. The press was protected so that it could bare the secrets of government and inform the people." (*New York Times v. United States*, June 30, 1971)

In covering the Kennedy assassination, the media abrogated their responsibility to reveal the deceptions and secrets of government. Instead, the media obligingly participated in the government's covering up of evidence.

How can a democracy have an enlightened citizenry if the actions of government are kept secret? To what extent can our society function as a democracy if our government lies to us and the news media perpetuate those lies?

"If a nation expects to be ignorant and free, in a state of civilization, it expects what never was and never will be."

— Thomas Jefferson
Letter to Charles Yancey
January 6, 1816

Document 1: **Dealey Plaza 1991**

Stewart Galanor

1. President Kennedy at Fatal Shot
2. Abraham Zapruder
3. Smoke
4. Railroad Workers
5. James Tague
6. Bullet Mark on Curb

Document 2: **Dealey Plaza Circa 1965**

Photographer Unknown

1. President Kennedy at Fatal Shot
2. Abraham Zapruder
3. Smoke
4. Railroad Workers
5. James Tague
6. Bullet Mark on Curb
7. Steam Pipe

Document 3: **Goatskin Test**

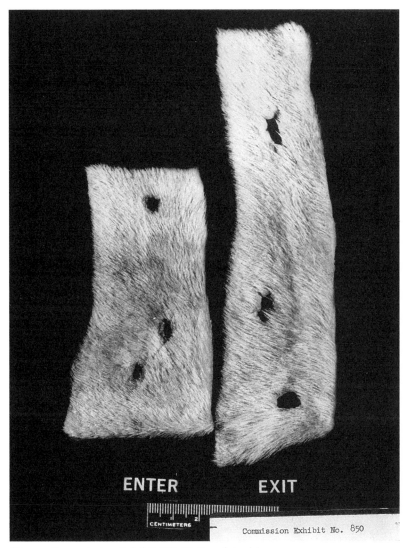

ENTER   EXIT

Commission Exhibit No. 850

Warren Commission Exhibit 850, National Archives.

Despite the Warren Commission's assurance to the contrary, entrance and exit wounds on the goatskin are easily distinguished from each other.

Document 4: **1964 FBI Reenactment of Assassination**

Left FBI agent is stand-in for President Kennedy.
Right FBI agent is stand-in for Governor Connally.

Document 5: **Autopsy Description Sheet**

The location of the back wound, which is lower than the throat wound, is inconsistent with a shot from the Book Depository Building. Dr. James Boswell, the autopsy pathologist who made out the Description Sheet, said it was just an approximation. The actual location of the back wound at the base of the neck is given by the figures adjacent to the diagram.

Document 6: **President Kennedy's Jacket**

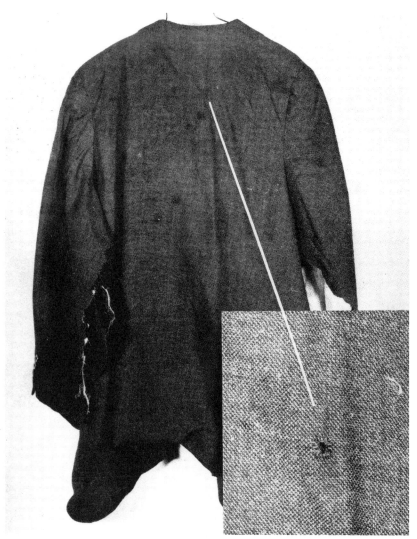

Warren Commission Document 107, Exhibit 59, National Archives.

Bullet hole is about 6 inches below the top of the collar and 2 inches to the right of the midline seam of the jacket. (2H365)

Document 7: **President Kennedy's Shirt**

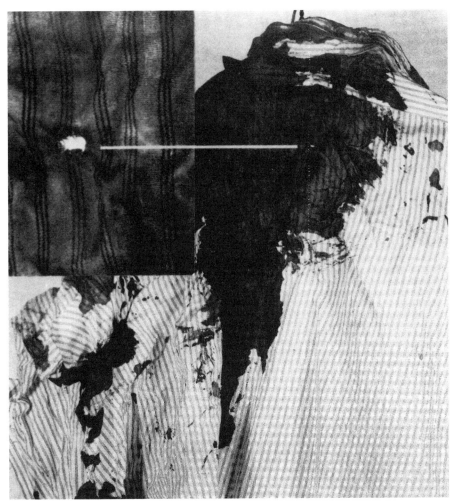

Warren Commission Document 107, Exhibit 60, National Archives.

Bullet hole is about 6 inches below the top of the collar and 2 inches to the right of the midline seam of the shirt. (2H365)

Document 8: **Death Certificate**

29. NAME

John Fitzgerald Kennedy

30. SUMMARY OF FACTS RELATING TO DEATH:

President John Fitzgerald Kennedy, while riding in the motorcade in Dallas, Texas, on November 22, 1963, and at approximately 12:30 p.m., was struck in the head by an assassin's bullet and a second wound occurred in the posterior back at about the level of the third thoracic vertebra. The wound was shattering in type causing a fragmentation of the skull and evulsion of three particles of the skull at time of the impact, with resulting maceration of the right hemisphere of the brain. The President was rushed to Parkland Memorial Hospital, and was immediately under the care of a team of physicians at the hospital under the direction of a neurosurgeon, Kemp Clark. I arrived at the hospital approximately five minutes after the President and immediately went to the emergency room. It was evident that the wound was of such severity that it was bound to be fatal. Breathing was noted at the time of arrival at the hospital by several members of the Secret Service. Emergency measures were employed immediately including intravenous fluid and blood. The President was pronounced dead at 1:00 p.m. by Dr. Clark and was verified by me.

31. DISPOSITION OF REMAINS

To the White House, Washington, D.C.

32.

DATE SIGNED November 23, 1963   SIGNATURE   George Gregory Burkley   RADM   (MC)

Physician to the President   (Rank)

33.

APPROVED: COURT OF INQUIRY OR BOARD OF INVESTIGATION _____ BE HELD.

(will or will not)

DATE SIGNED _____ SIGNATURE _____   USN

(Commanding Officer)   (Rank)

JFK Records Group 272, Warrren Commission Records, Entry 52, National Archives.

The President's physician Dr. Burkley placed the back wound at the level of the third thoracic vertebra.

Document 9: **Warren Commission Drawing**

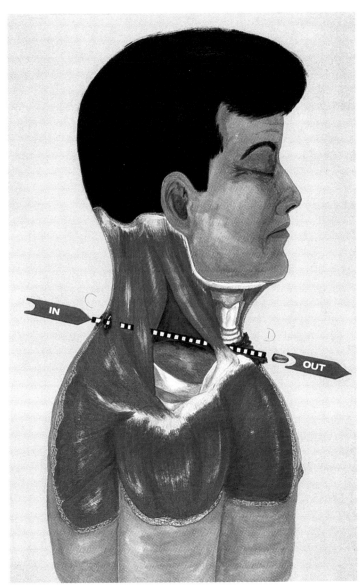

Warren Commission Exhibit 385, National Archives.

The Warren Commission suppressed the autopsy X-rays and photographs and instead used as evidence the three drawings, Documents 9, 10 and 11.

Document 10: **Warren Commission Drawing**

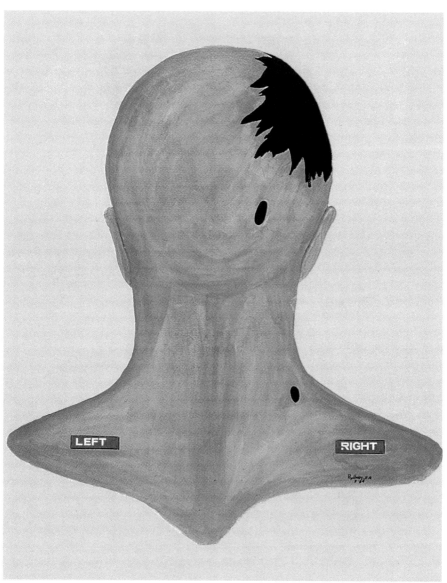

Warren Commission Exhibit 386, National Archives.

Document 11: **Warren Commission Drawing**

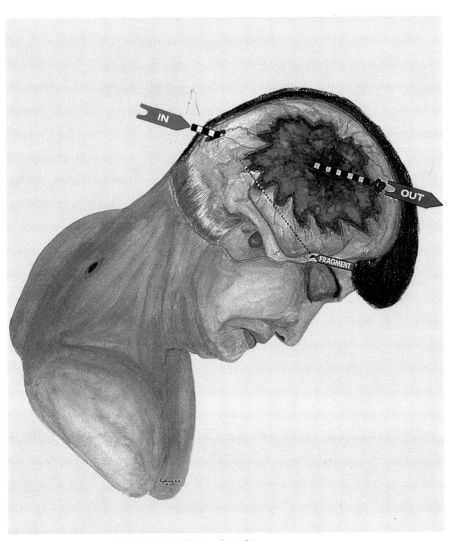

Warren Commission Exhibit 388, National Archives.

Document 12: **Alleged Autopsy Photograph**

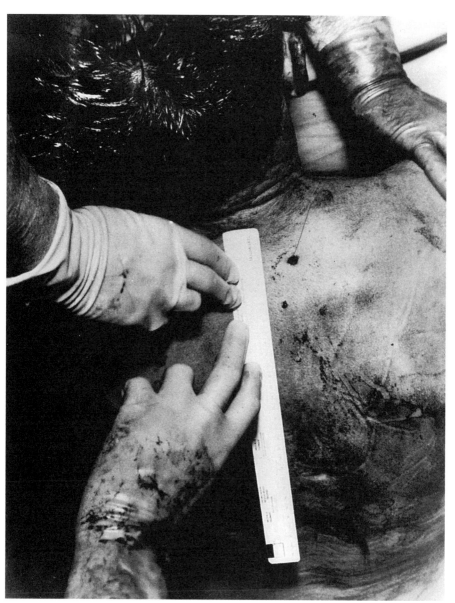

This photograph first appeared in *Best Evidence* by David Lifton who acquired it from Secret Service photographer James Fox.

Document 13: **Medical Illustration of Spine and Trachea**

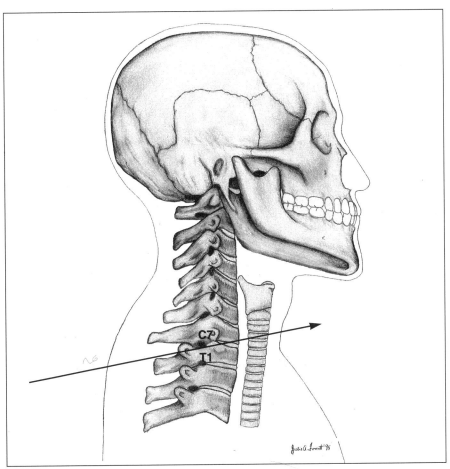

Illustration by Julie Foont, Illustrator for *The Fundamentals of Operative Neurosurgery,* Thieme Medical and Scientific Publishers, 1999.

A bullet striking the President's back at the level of the first thoracic vertebra (T1), and then exiting the throat between the levels of the third and fourth tracheal rings, would have to be rising, a path which is inconsistent with a shot from the sixth floor of the Book Depository Building.

Document 14: *NOVA* Computer Simulation

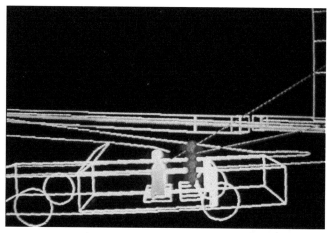

Since the President's back wound was anatomically lower than his throat wound, his wounds did not line up with a shot from the sixth floor of the Book Depository.

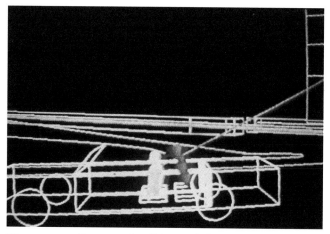

Thus, according to the House Select Committee on Assassinations and to *NOVA*, the President must have bent forward just before he was shot. ("Who Shot President Kennedy?," *NOVA*, November, 1988) However, none of the films and photographs show the President bending forward.

Document 15: **Zapruder Film Frame 228**

Abraham Zapruder

Zapruder Frame 228 shows that the President was not bending forward moments after he was shot in the throat.

Document 16: **Dr. McClelland's Drawing**

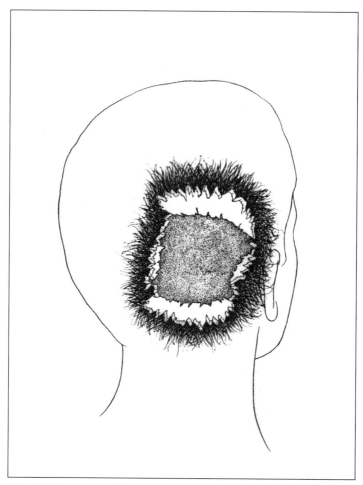

Dr. Robert McClelland's drawing, made for Josiah Thompson's *Six Seconds in Dallas*, represents what doctors at Parkland Hospital observed to be the approximate size and location of President Kennedy's head wound. It was not drawn to depict the edges of the wound or the exact destruction of the skull and brain.

Document 17: **Zapruder Film Frame 312**

Abraham Zapruder

Frame 312 of the Zapruder film is the frame before the fatal shot.

Document 18: Warren Commission Drawing and Zapruder Frame 312

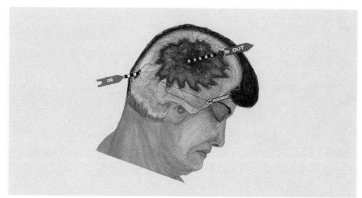

Document 10

Zapruder Frame 312

When the Warren Commission Drawing (Document 10) is turned so that President Kennedy is in the same position shown in frame 312 of the Zapruder Film, the path of the bullet is rising which is inconsistent with a shot from the sixth floor of the Book Depository Building.

Document 19: **HSCA Drawing**

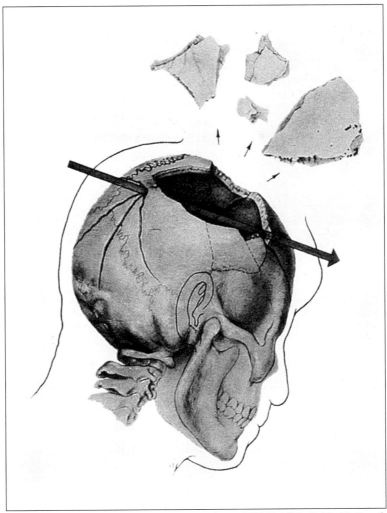

House Select Committee on Assassinations, JFK Exhibit F-66, National Archives.

President Kennedy's head wounds according to the Clark Panel and the House Select Committee on Assassination.

Document 20: **Location of Skull Bones**

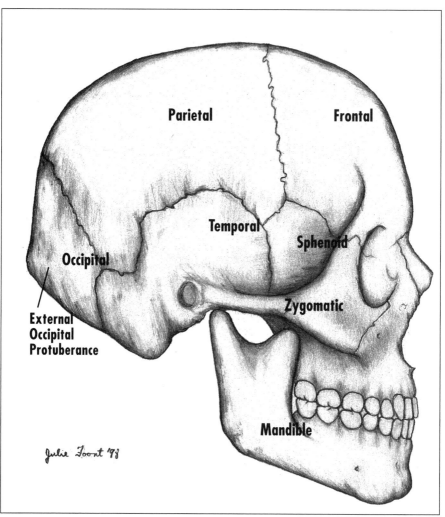

Illustration by Julie Foont, Illustrator for *The Fundamentals of Operative Neurosurgery*, Thieme Medical and Scientific Publishers, 1999.

Document 21: **Two Motorcycle Officers**

Zapruder Film, Frame 242, National Archives.

The fatal shot splattered two motorcycle officers, Bobby Hargis and B.J. Martin, with pieces of skull and blood and brain matter. Hargis was struck so hard that he said, "I thought at first I might have been hit." *New York Daily News*, November 24, 1963.

Document 22: **FBI Reenactment of Assassination**

At Zapruder Frame 210

At Zapruder Frame 222

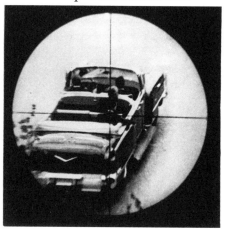

Warren Commission Exhibits 893 and 894,
National Archives.

The FBI failed to use the Presidential Limousine in their reenactment.
Yet the Warren Commission claimed the reenactment supported the
Single Bullet Theory, even though, when viewed through a telescopic
sight from the sixth floor window, the wounds of the President and the
Governor did not line up.

Document 23: **Three Bullets**

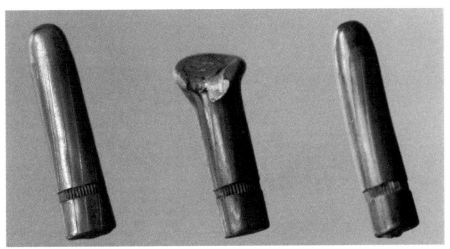

Stewart Galanor

Left: Bullet that Warren Commission claimed struck both
President Kennedy and Governor Connally, the magic bullet.
Warren Commission Exhibit 399, National Archives.

Center: Bullet fired through a cadaver's wrist.
Warren Commission Exhibit 856, National Archives.

Right: Bullet fired into cotton.
Warren Commission Exhibit 572, National Archives.

Book Depository: *AP/World Wide Photo*
Rifle Test Tower: Warren Commission Exhibit 579, National Archives.

The Warren Commission rifle test was conducted from a 30 foot tower at the Army's Ballistics Research Laboratory at the Aberdeen Proving Grounds. The sixth floor window of the Book Depository Building is 60 feet above the ground.

Document 25: **Three Stationary Targets**

Warren Commission Exhibit 580, National Archives.

The view of the three stationary targets from the rifle test tower.

Document 26: **One of Three Rifle Test Targets**

Warren Commission Exhibit 583, National Archives.

Although markmen hit this target five times, none of the shots hit the head or neck region.

Document 27: **Grassy Knoll Within 20 Seconds of Assassination**

Wilma Bond

Document 28: **Associated Press Dispatch by James Altgens**

B133DN
        WITH KENNEDY (250)
     (EDITOR'S NOTE--JAMES W. ALTGENS, AN ASSOCIATED PRESS PHOTOGRAPHER,
WAS NEAR THE PRESIDENT'S CAR WHEN HE WAS SHOT TODAY.)

BY JAMES W. ALTGENS
ASSOCIATED PRESS STAFF PHOTOGRAPHER
     DALLAS, TEX, NOV.22 (AP)-THERE WAS A BURST OF NOISE--THE SECOND
ONE I HEARD--AND PIECES OF FLESH APPEARED TO FLY FROM PRESIDENT
KENNEDY'S CAR.
     BLOOD COVERED THE WHOLE LEFT SIDE OF HIS HEAD.
     MRS. KENNEDY SAW WHAT HAD HAPPENED TO HER HUSBAND. SHE GRABBED HIM
EXCLAIMING, "OH, NO!"
     THE CAR'S DRIVER REALIZED WHAT HAD HAPPENED AND ALMOST AS IF BY
REFLEX SPEEDED UP TOWARD THE STEMMONS EXPRESSWAY. THERE SEEMED TO BE
UTTER CONFUSION.
     ONE MOTORCYCLE OFFICER RAN HIS CYCLE INTO THE CURB, ALMOST FALLING
OFF.
     POLICE CAME FROM EVERYWHERE AS THE PRESIDENT'S CAR DISAPPEARED FROM
SIGHT.
     AT FIRST I THOUGHT THE SHOTS CAME FROM THE OPPOSITE SIDE OF THE
STREET. I RAN OVER THERE TO SEE IF I COULD GET SOME PICTURES. BUT IT
TURNED OUT TO BE JUST MORE CONFUSION. POLICE RAN IN ALL DIRECTIONS IN
SEARCH OF THE ASSASSIN.

B134DN
     I DID NOT KNOW UNTIL LATER WHERE THE SHOTS CAME FROM. I WAS ON THE
OPPOSITE SIDE OF THE PRESIDENT'S CAR FROM THE GUNMAN. HE MIGHT HAVE HIT
ME.
     THE MOTORCADE WAS MOVING ALONG IN ROUTINE FASHION UNTIL THERE WAS A
NOISE LIKE FIREWORKS POPPING. I SNAPPED A PICTURE OF THE MOTORCADE
AT JUST ABOUT THAT TIME. STILL UNAWARE OF WHAT WAS HAPPENING.
     I CRANKED MY CAMERA FOR ANOTHER SHOT. THE PROCESSION STILL MOVED
ALONG SLOWLY. THEN CAME THE SECOND BURST OF NOISE.
     ORIGINALLY I HAD PLANNED TO BE ON TOP OF A TRIPLE OVERPASS TO MAKE
A SCENIC PICTURE OF THE DALLAS SKYLINE WHEN THE MOTORCADE PASSED.
BUT POLICE WOULDN'T LET ME STAY THERE--THE OVER PASS BELONGS TO A
RAILROAD.
     SO I MOVED TO THE CORNER OF HOUSTON AND MAIN STREETS, MADE A COUPLE
OF PICTURES AND RAN DOWNHILL TO GET IN FRONT OF THE MOTORCADE AGAIN.
THIS PUT ME IN PLACE FOR THE PICTURES OF THE PRESIDENT BEING STRUCK
DOWN.
     JA/JJ749PCS

AP/Wide World Photo

Document 29: Secret Service Agent Glen Bennett Looking Off to Right

Phillip Willis

Left Arrow: President Kennedy
Right Arrow: Secret Service Agent Glen Bennett

In the photograph Secret Service Agent Glen Bennett is looking off to the right moments before President Kennedy, according to the Warren Commission, is struck in the back. Yet Bennett claimed "I saw a shot that hit the Boss about four inches down from the right shoulder." Other photographs taken after the President is shot show Bennet still looking off to the right. (James Altgens, *AP/Wide World Photo*)

Document 30: Backyard Photograph

LIFE

LEE
OSWALD

with the
weapons he
used to kill
President Kennedy
and
Officer Tippit

FEBRUARY 21 · 1964 · 25¢

Life Magazine

Document 31: **Mannlicher-Carcano**

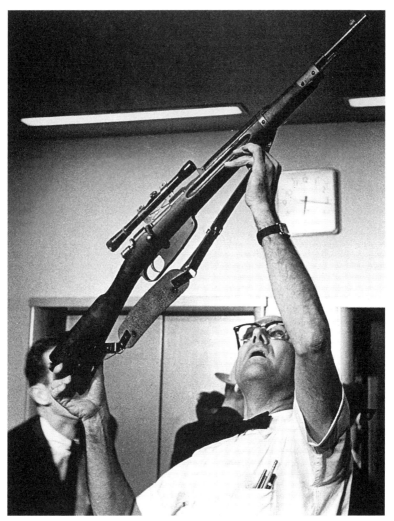

Warren Commission Exhibit 339, National Archives.

Lieutenant Day of the Dallas Police displaying a Mannlicher-Carcano to the press.

Document 32: Backyard Photograph

Newsweek, March 2, 1964

Document 33: **Chins**

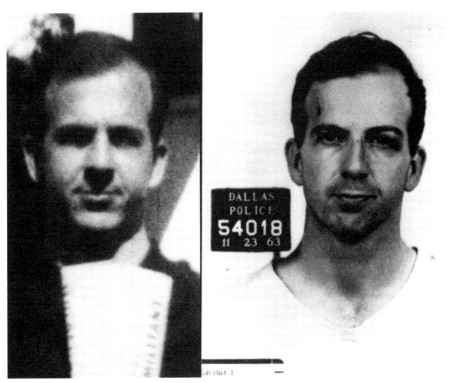

Left: Blowup of backyard photograph.

Right: Warren Commission, Aubrey Lewis Exhibit, National Archives.

Document 34: **FBI Attempt to Duplicate Shadows**

Warren Commission Exhibit 748, National Archives.

Document 35: **The London Times Unable to Duplicate Shadows**

The London Times, October 9, 1966.

Document 36: **Silhouette Found in Dallas Police Files**

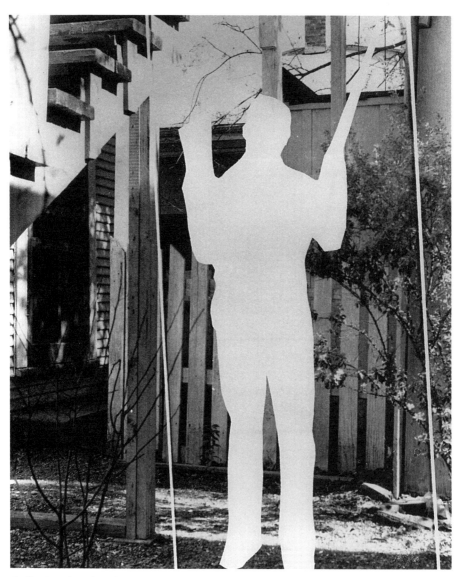

Dallas Municipal Archives and Records Center, 91-001/288

Document 37: **Letter From U. S. Post Office Department**

POST OFFICE DEPARTMENT
BUREAU OF OPERATIONS
WASHINGTON, D.C. 20260

WT/sd

May 3, 1966

Mr. Stewart Galanor
3900 Greystone Avenue
Riverdale, New York 10463

Dear Mr. Galanor:

In reply to your inquiry of May 3, the following regulations referred to were in effect at all postal installations in March 1963.

Section 846.53h, of the Postal Manual, provides that the third portion of box rental applications, identifying persons other than the applicant authorized to receive mail, must be retained for two years after the box is closed.

Section 355.111b(4), prescribes that mail addressed to a person at a post office box, who is not authorized to receive mail, shall be endorsed "addressee unknown", and returned to the sender where possible.

Sincerely yours,

Ralph R. Rea
Director
Special Services Branch

Document 38: **U. S. Post Office Regulations**

846.5 RECORDS RETAINED FOR PERIODS OTHER THAN 1 YEAR

.51 Dispose of all records maintained at post offices after 1 year except those covered in 846.42 and 846.43 and those in the following categories:

.52 International Mail   *Retention Period*

a. International mail schedules_____ 3 years.

b. International air and steamer mail files:
   (1) International letter bills_____ 6 years.
   (2) Steamer arrival and dispatch logs, bulle- 4 years.
       tins of verification, registry receipts,
       check sheets, waybills, trip tickets, and
       records pertaining to delivery and receipt
       of international mail and military mail.

c. Universal postal statistics_____ 8 years.

.53 Postal Procedures

a. Delivery receipts for firearms, and statements 4 years.
   by shippers of firearms (Forms 2162, 1508).

b. Applications and permits for special mailing Place in inactive file on
   privileges, mailing without affixing postage, termination or cancella-
   use of precanceled stamps, distribution of   tion. Start new inactive
   business reply cards, use of meter postage,   file each year. Destroy 3
   mailing under 2d and 3d class, etc.   years after close of year
                                                 in which terminated or
                                                 cancelled.

c. Marked copies of publications admitted as 6 months.
   second class mail matter.

d. Patron change of address files_____ 2 years.

e. Case examination records (Form 3990) _____ Place on right side of official
                                                personnel folder upon
                                                separation of employee.

f. Registered, insured, COD, and certified mail 2 years.
   receipts, and delivery and dispatch records
   (such as Forms 3805, 3806, 3824, 3867, 3877,
   3896).

g. COD Tags as money order applications, and 2 years after quarter of
   other delivery office COD records (such as   money order issue or 2
   Form 3814 series, 3821, 3822).   years after other disposi-
                                                tion of case.

h. Box rental applications and control cards 2 years after close of box.
   showing payment.

i. Route inspection reports:
   (1) Made annually or more frequently_____ 2 years.
   (2) Made less frequently than annually_____ 5 years.

j. Meter mailings, 2d-class mailings, statement 3 years.
   of mailing matter with permit imprints, receipt for postage meter setting, and weighing
   and dispatch certificates (such as Forms 3541,
   3542, 3602, 3603, 3607, 3609, 3610).

k. Publishers statement of ownership manage- 2 years.
   ment and circulation.

l. Patron application for U.S. savings bonds___ 2 years.

m. Rural route file folders:
   (1) Right side material_____ Retain.
   (2) Left side material_____ 1 year.

Document 39: **Warren Commission's Star Witness Howard Brennan**

Warren Commission Exhibit 477, National Archives.

Photograph of Howard Brennan, taken four days before he appeared before the Warren Commisssion, shows where he was sitting on November 22, 1963. Brennan testified he observed Oswald shoot at President Kennedy from the sixth floor window (circle labeled A).

Document 40: **Officer Marion Baker Encounters Oswald in Lunchroom**

September 23, 1964
Dallas, Texas

I, Marion L. Baker, do hereby furnish this voluntary signed statement to Richard J. Burnett who has identified himself to me as a Special Agent of the Federal Bureau of Investigation.

I am employed as an officer with the Dallas police department and was so employed as of November 22, 1963.

On the early afternoon of that day after hearing what sounded to me to be bullet shots, I entered the Texas School Book Depository Building on the northwest corner of Elm and Houston Streets in downtown Dallas.

I had entered that building in an effort to determine if the shots might have come from that building.

On the second ~~which floor~~ floor MLB, where the lunch room is located, I saw a man standing in the lunch room. ~~drinking a coke~~ MLB. He was alone in the lunch room at that time.

~~I saw no one else in the vicinity of the lunch room at this time.~~

M. L. Baker

Warren Commission Exhibit 3076, National Archives.

Document 41: **Ruby Fails as FBI Informant**

OFFICE OF THE DIRECTOR

Commission No. *1052*

UNITED STATES DEPARTMENT OF JUSTICE

FEDERAL BUREAU OF INVESTIGATION

WASHINGTON 25, D. C.

June 9, 1964

BY COURIER SERVICE

Honorable J. Lee Rankin
General Counsel
The President's Commission
200 Maryland Avenue, Northeast
Washington, D. C. 20002

Dear Mr. Rankin:

Your letter of June 1, 1964, requesting summaries of FBI reports with regard to ten named persons and certain information regarding the contact by Special Agent Charles W. Flynn with Jack L. Ruby on March 11, 1959, is herewith acknowledged.

As you were advised by my letter of February 27, 1964, Jack Ruby was contacted by Special Agent Charles W. Flynn of the Dallas Office on March 11, 1959, in view of his position as a night club operator who might have knowledge of the criminal element in Dallas. The purpose of this contact was to determine whether or not Ruby did have such knowledge, and if so, if he would be willing to furnish information to this Bureau. Ruby was advised of the FBI's jurisdiction in criminal matters, and he expressed a <u>willingness to furnish information</u>. A personal description of Ruby was obtained by Special Agent Flynn on the occasion of this contact on March 11, 1959, but <u>no information</u> or other results were obtained. Between March 11, 1959, and October 2, 1959, Ruby was contacted on eight other occasions, but he furnished <u>no information whatever</u> and further contacts with him were discontinued.

Warren Commission Document 1052, National Archives.

Document 42: **Right Lateral Autopsy X-ray of President's Head**

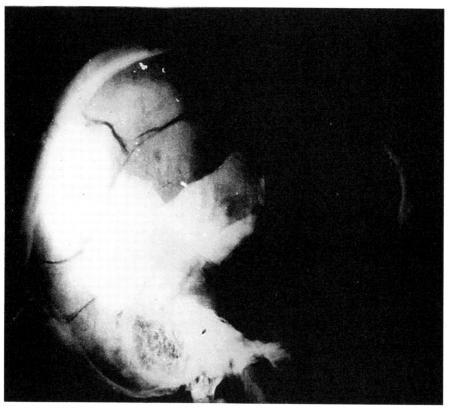

House Select Committee on Assassinations, JFK Exhibit F-52, National Archives.

Document 43: **X-ray of President Kennedy During His Lifetime**

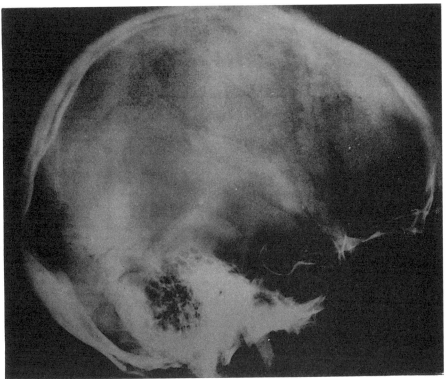

House Select Committee on Assassinations, JFK Exhibit F-297, National Archives.

Document 44: **Frontal Autopsy X-ray of President's Head**

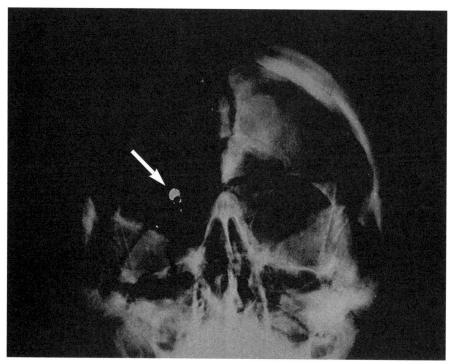

House Select Committee on Assassinations, JFK Exhibit F-55, National Archives.

Document 45: **Death of the Lone Assassin Theory**

**Location of
Throat Wound**

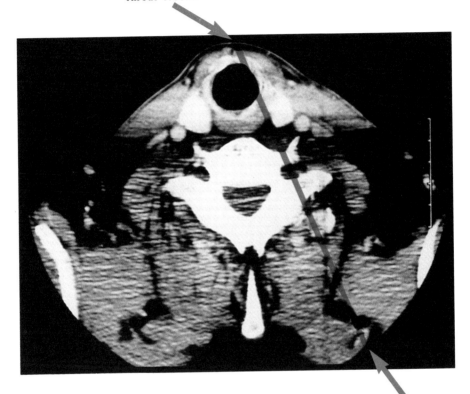

**Location of
Back Wound
at Neck Level**

The CAT Scan was taken of a patient at Eisenhower Memorial Hospital with upper chest and neck dimensions the same as President Kennedy's. Dr. Mantik took the CAT Scan at the base of the neck at the level of the seventh cervical vertebra. ("Optical Density Measurements of the JFK Autopsy X-rays and a New Observation Based on the Chest X-ray" by David Mantik, *Assassination Science*, edited by James Fetzer. Chicago: Catfeet Press, 1998)

Document 46: **Autopsy Notes Destroyed**

U. S. NAVAL MEDICAL SCHOOL
NATIONAL NAVAL MEDICAL CENTER
BETHESDA, MARYLAND 20014

In reply refer to

24 November 1963

C-E-R-T-I-F-I-C-A-T-E

I, James J. Humes, certify that I have destroyed by burning certain preliminary draft notes relating to Naval Medical School Autopsy Report A63-272 and have officially transmitted all other papers related to this report to higher authority.

J. J. HUMES
CDR, MC, USN

Warren Commission Exhibit 397, National Archives.

ZAPRUDER FRAMES

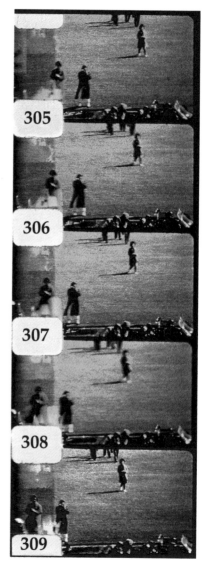

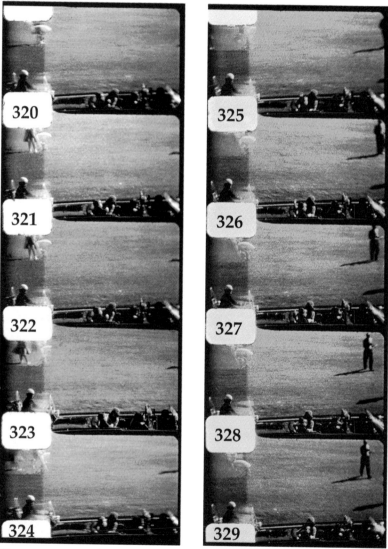

The sequence of frames 290 to 329 was assembled from individual slides stored in the National Archives.

216 WITNESSES

WITNESS	ORIGIN OF SHOTS	CITATION
Adams, Victoria	Knoll	6H388
Allen, J. B.	Could Not Tell	22H601
Altgens, James	Knoll	C68
Arce, Danny	Knoll	6H365
Arnold, Carolyn	Not Asked	22H635
Ault, Cecil	Could Not Tell	24H534
Baker, Marrion	Depository	3H246
Baker, Virgie	Knoll	7H510
Barclay, Malcolm	Not Asked	26H552
Barnett, Welcome	Depository	7H541
Bennett, Glen	Depository	24H542
Berry, Jane	Knoll	CD5
Betzner, Hugh	Could Not Tell	24H200
Bishop, Curtis	Not Asked	22H834
Bond, Wilma	Not Asked	CD735
Boone, Eugene	Knoll	19H508
Bowers, Lee	Knoll & Depository	6H287
Brehm, Charles	Depository	22H837
Brennen, Howard	Depository	3H143
Brown, Earle	Depository	6H234
Burkley, George	Not Asked	22H93
Burns, Doris	Knoll	6H399
Cabell, Earle	Depository	7H479
Cabell, Mrs. Earle	Depository	7H486
Calvery, Gloria	Not Asked	22H638
Campbell, Ochus	Knoll	22H638
Carr, Richard	Knoll	CD329
Carter, Clifton	Not Asked	7H474
Chism, John	Knoll	24H525

WITNESS	ORIGIN OF SHOTS	CITATION
Chism, Marvin	Knoll	19H472
Clark, Rose	Not Asked	24H533
Clay, Billie	Not Asked	22H641
Connally, John	Depository	4H129
Connally, Mrs. John	Depository	4H149
Couch, Malcolm	Depository	6H157
Cowsert, Ewell	Could Not Tell	22H836
Craig, Roger	Could Not Tell	6H263
Crawford, James	Knoll	6H173
Curry, Jesse	Knoll	23H913
Darnell, James	Not Asked	CD7
Davis, Avery	Knoll	22H642
Davis, George	Not Asked	22H837
Dean, Ruth	Depository	22H839
Decker, Bill	Knoll	23H913
Denham, W. H.	Could Not Tell	22H599
Dickerson, Mary	Not Asked	22H644
Dillard, Tom	Depository	6H165
Dodd, Richard	Knoll	RTJ
Dolan, John	Could Not Tell	CD205
Dorman, Elsie	Elsewhere	22H644
Dougherty, Jack	Depository	6H379
Downey, William	Not Asked	26H551
Dragoo, Betty	Not Asked	22H645
Edwards, Robert	Could Not Tell	6H200
Elkins, Harold	Knoll	19H540
Euins, Amos	Depository	2H203
Faulkner, Jack	Not Asked	19H511
Fischer, Ronald	Knoll	6H195
Foster, Betty	Not Asked	22H647
Foster, James	Depository	6H251
Franzen, Jack	Could Not Tell	22H840
Franzen, Mrs. Jack	Knoll	24H525
Frazier, Wesley	Knoll	2H234
Garner, Dorothy	Knoll	22H648
Givens, Charles	Not Asked	6H345
Greer, William	Not Asked	2H112
Hargis, Bobby	Could Not Tell	6H294
Harkness, D. V.	Could Not Tell	6H309
Hawkins, Peggy	Knoll	CD897
Haygood, Clyde	Not Asked	6H298

WITNESS	ORIGIN OF SHOTS	CITATION
Henderson, Ruby	Not Asked	24H524
Hendrix, Georgia	Not Asked	22H649
Hester, Beatrice	Could Not Tell	24H523
Hester, Charles	Depository	19H478
Hester, Mrs. Charles	Could Not Tell	CD7
Hickey, George	Depository	18H765
Hicks, Karan	Not Asked	22H650
Hill, Clinton	Depository	2H138
Hill, Jean	Knoll	6H212
Hine, Geneva	Depository	6H395
Holland, S. M.	Knoll	6H243
Hollies, Mary	Not Asked	22H652
Holmes, Harry	Could Not Tell	7H292
Holt, Gloria	Not Asked	22H652
Hooker, Jeanette	Could Not Tell	24H533
Hopson, Yola	Elsewhere	24H521
Hudson, Emmett	Depository	7H560
Hughes, Carol	Not Asked	22H654
Hughes, Robert	Not Asked	25H873
Jacks, Hurchel	Depository	18H801
Jackson, Robert	Knoll & Depository	2H162
Jacob, Stella	Not Asked	22H655
Jarman, James	Depository	3H198
Johns, Thomas	Not Asked	18H774
Johnson, Clemon	Not Asked	22H836
Johnson, Judy	Not Asked	22H656
Johnson, Lyndon	Could Not Tell	5H562
Johnson, Mrs. Lyndon	Depository	5H565
Jones, C. M.	Not Asked	19H512
Jones, Carl Edward	Could Not Tell	22H657
Kantor, Seth	Not Asked	15H74
Kellerman, Roy	Depository	2H75
Kennedy, Mrs. John F.	Not Asked	5H180
King, W. K.	Not Asked	22H601
Kinney, Samuel	Not Asked	18H732
Kivett, Jerry	Depository	18H778
Kounas, Dolores	Knoll	22H659
Lacy, James	Depository	CD897
Landis, Paul	Knoll & Depository	18H759
Lawrence, Patricia	Depository	22H841
Lawson, Winston	Could Not Tell	4H353
Lewis, Carlus	Could Not Tell	22H602

WITNESS	ORIGIN OF SHOTS	CITATION
Lewis, Clinton	Not Asked	19H526
Lewis, Roy	Depository	22H661
Lovelady, Billy	Knoll	6H338
Mabra, W. W.	Not Asked	19H541
Martin, B. J.	Could Not Tell	6H289
Martin, John, Jr.	Depository	CD897
McCully, Judith	Could Not Tell	22H663
McCurley, A. D.	Not Asked	19H514
McIntyre, William	Could Not Tell	18H747
McVey, Oscar	Elsewhere	CD5
Miller, Austin	Knoll	19H485
Millican, A. J.	Knoll & Depository	19H486
Mitchell, Mary	Not Asked	6H175
Molina, Joe	Knoll	6H371
Mooney, Luke	Knoll	3H281
Mooneyham, Lillian	Not Asked	24H531
Moore, T. E.	Depository	24H534
Moorman, Mary	Could Not Tell	22H838
Muchmore, Marie	Could Not Tell	CD735
Mudd, F. Lee	Depository	24H538
Murphy, Joe	Could Not Tell	6H259
Murphy, Thomas	Knoll	22H835
Nelson, Ruth	Not Asked	22H665
Nelson, Sharon	Not Asked	22H665
Newman, Frances	Not Asked	22H842
Newman, Jean	Knoll	22H843
Newman, William	Knoll	19H490
Nix, Orville	Knoll	RTJ
Norman, Harold	Depository	3H191
O'Brien, Lawrence	Could Not Tell	7H464
O'Donnell, Kenneth	Knoll	C68
Oxford, J. L.	Not Asked	19H530
Parker, Roberta	Knoll	CD205
Paternostro, Samuel	Knoll & Depository	24H536
Piper, Eddie	Depository	6H386
Player, Charles	Not Asked	19H515
Potter, Nolan	Could Not Tell	22H834
Powell, James	Not Asked	CD206
Powers, David	Knoll	7H473
Price, J. C.	Knoll	RTJ
Ready, John	Depository	18H750

WITNESS	ORIGIN OF SHOTS	CITATION
Reed, Carol	Not Asked	22H668
Reed, Martha	Could Not Tell	22H669
Reese, Madie	Elsewhere	22H669
Reid, Mrs. Robert	Depository	3H273
Reid, Robert	Not Asked	24H532
Reilly, Frank	Knoll	6H230
Rich, Joe	Not Asked	18H800
Richey, Bonnie	Not Asked	22H671
Roberts, Emory	Could Not Tell	18H739
Romack, James	Depository	6H280
Rowland, Arnold	Knoll	2H165
Rowland, Barbara	Could Not Tell	6H184
Sanders, Pauline	Depository	22H844
Shelley, William	Knoll	6H329
Shields, Edwards	Not Asked	7H393
Simmons, James	Knoll	RTJ
Sitzman, Marilyn	Elsewhere	19H535
Skelton, Royce	Could Not Tell	6H237
Slack, Garland	Knoll & Depository	26H364
Smith, Edgar	Knoll	7H568
Smith, Joe Marshall	Knoll	7H535
Smith, L. C.	Not Asked	19H516
Smith, Ruth	Not Asked	CD206
Solon, John	Not Asked	24H535
Sorrels, Forrest	Knoll	7H346
Springer, Pearl	Not Asked	24H523
Stansbery, Joyce	Not Asked	22H674
Stanton, Sarah	Could Not Tell	22H675
Styles, Sandra	Could Not Tell	22H676
Summers, Malcolm	Knoll	19H500
Sweatt, Allan	Depository	19H531
Tague, James	Knoll	7H556
Taylor, Warren	Depository	18H782
Thornton, Betty	Not Asked	22H677
Thornton, Ruth	Not Asked	24H537
Todd, L. C.	Not Asked	19H543
Truly, Roy	Knoll	3H221
Underwood, James	Depository	6H169
Viles, Lloyd	Not Asked	22H678
Walters, Ralph	Not Asked	19H505
Walther, Carolyn	Could Not Tell	24H522

WITNESS	ORIGIN OF SHOTS	CITATION
Walthers, Buddy	Not Asked	7H544
Watson, Jack	Not Asked	19H522
Weatherford, Harry	Knoll	19H502
Weaver, Jack	Not Asked	CD329
Weitzman, Seymour	Knoll	24H228
Westbrook, Karen	Not Asked	22H679
Whitaker, Lupe	Not Asked	22H681
Williams, Bonnie	Depository	3H175
Williams, Mary	Not Asked	22H682
Williams, Otis	Knoll	22H683
Willis, Linda	Could Not Tell	7H498
Willis, Phillip	Depository	7H497
Willis, Mrs. Philip	Not Asked	CD1245
Wilson, Steven	Knoll	22H685
Winborn, Walter	Knoll	C60
Wiseman, John	Not Asked	19H535
Woodward, Mary	Knoll	C71
Worrell, James	Depository	2H193
Wright, Milton	Not Asked	18H802
Yarborough, Ralph	Depository	7H440
Youngblood, Rufus	Depository	2H150
Zapruder, Abraham	Knoll	CD87

Warren Commission documents not published in the 26 Volumes were deposited in the JFK Records Group at the National Archives and are cited by their CD number. CD5 means Warren Commission Document 5.

C12 means see *Cover-up*, page 12, for the citation.

RTJ means the witness was interviewed by Mark Lane in the film *Rush to Judgment* which is available on home video from MPI, Chicago.

An excellent map of the location of over 300 witnesses to the assassination is available from Craig Ciccone, Detroit, MI.

CITATIONS

Two major investigations of the assassination of President Kennedy were conducted by the U. S. Government. The Warren Commission released its report at the end of September 1964. Two months later the 26 Volumes of Testimony and Exhibits on which the Warren Report was supposedly based were released. The House Select Committee on Assassinations released its report at the end of March 1979, along with 12 volumes of supporting evidence.

Citations from these two investigations and other sources are given in the text. Nearly all the evidence for a conspiracy and a cover-up of the assassination was assembled by the Warren Commission and stored in the National Archives in Washington, D.C.

WR123 means page 123 of the *Report of the President's Commission on the Assassination of President John F. Kennedy*, which is known as the Warren Report. It was published on September 27, 1964.

2H345 means page 345 of volume 2 of the *Hearings Before the President's Commission on the Assassination of President Kennedy*, which is known as the 26 Volumes of Hearings and Exhibits of the Warren Commission, or more simply the 26 Volumes. They were published on November 23, 1964.

HSCA Report 123 means page 123 of the *Report of the Select Committee on Assassinations, U.S. House of Representatives*. It was published on March 30, 1979.

2HSCA345 means page 345 of volume 2 of the *Hearings of the House Select Committee on Assassinations*. The 12 volumes were published in 1979.

These four government works can be found in the main library of most cities and at university libraries. They are also available on CD-ROM. The Warren Report is currently published by St. Martin's Press, New York City.

The Zapruder film is available on home video from MPI, Chicago.

Most of the documents mentioned in this book are stored in the National Archives.

ACKNOWLEDGMENTS

I am extremely grateful for the encouragement and support of Alan Siegel, Anita Mayo, Jesse Jones, Margaret Konikowski, Jim Neuberger, Richard Kraut, Ted Cohen, Ray Raphael, Joel Perlman, Bob Spiegelman, Robert Young, Barbara LaMonica, Gene Case, Tom Gatch, Stephen Gottlieb and Marc Farley.

The many trips I made to the National Archives would not have been possible without the help of Jim Collins and Nancy Michel. They provided valuable criticism and guidance at the book's inception.

Gary Mack and John Puff helped examine and locate many documents. Their extensive knowledge of the Zapruder film and other films and photographs of the assassination is extraordinary.

Marion Johnson arranged a screening at the National Archives of the Zapruder film in 1965.

Steven Hamilton, Martha Murphy, Ramona Oliver and Steven Tilley at the National Archives helped track down numerous documents.

Robert Krauss patiently answered my questions about rifles and ammunition.

David Lifton supplied excellent prints of the Zapruder film and made many incisive observations about the medical evidence and Oswald's background.

Patricia Taylor, David Starks, Lauren Meeker,
Matthew Schaenen, Milicent Cranor, Mary-Lis Uruena,
Tom Lyons, George Costello and Paul Burns read the
manuscript and each made many significant changes.

Helen Edersheim generously volunteered her time
and skills as copy editor.

In 1964 Ralph and Marlene Behrends and Mark Lane
taught me a great deal about finding and presenting
evidence, much of which found its way into *Rush to
Judgment* and now *Cover-up*.

Fred Daly polished many awkward passages and
made important contributions to virtually every page.

Finally, I wish to acknowledge the contribution of
my sister Janet, whose advice on the presentation of
evidence was invaluable.

BIBLIOGRAPHY

Epstein, Edward Jay. *Inquest: The Warren Commission and the Establishment of Truth.* New York: Bantam, 1966.

Lane, Mark. *Rush to Judgment.* New York: Holt, Rinehart & Winston, 1966.

Lifton, David. *Best Evidence: Disguise and Deception in the Assassination of John F. Kennedy.* New York: Macmillan, 1981; Carroll & Graf, 1988.

Melanson, Philip. *Spy Saga: Lee Harvey Oswald and U.S. Intelligence.* New York: Praeger, 1990.

Newman, John. *Oswald and the CIA.* New York: Carroll & Graf, 1995.

Posner, Gerald. *Case Closed.* New York: Random House, 1993.

Scheim, David. *Contract on America: The Mafia Murders of John and Robert Kennedy.* New York: Shapolsky Books, 1988.

Thompson, Josiah. *Six Seconds in Dallas: A Microstudy of the Kennedy Assassination.* New York: Bernard Geis Associates, 1967.

Trask, Richard. *Pictures of the Pain.* Danvers, MA: Yeoman Press, 1994.

Weisberg, Harold. *Post Mortem.* Frederick, MD: Self-published, 1975.

INDEX